I want to express my extreme gratitude for having the opportunity to share my life with those special friends and family I grew up with. Too say the least, they truly helped to sculpt my character and my values, besides they were a lot fun to hang around with. Also, to my children, whom I love dearly, they were the inspiration for me to live up to the standards and morality of pursuing a righteous and rewarding life. And last but not least, my wife, my best friend, my soul mate. Thank you for sharing yourself and your life with me. It has truly been an honor. Oh ya, if you're ever rolling north or south on highway 41 and a foul sulfur odor attacks your nasal passages, you are passing by my hometown of Kaukauna. That odor is being emitted from a paper mill called Thilmanys, the largest employer in my hometown and when I was a kid and the wind had decided to send that foul smell to our address, I would always complain and my dad would always give me the same answer, "son that is the smell of money being made". Of all the hometowns that dot the American landscape, I am so glad I grew up in our little piece of heaven, Kaukauna Wisconsin. And P.S., every one of these stories is true, just embellished for your comedic enjoyment.

• • • •• •• ••• • • •• • ••

• • • •• • ˙ ˙ •• • • • • • •• • • •

• • • •• • ••• •• • • ••

I was told that the day I arrived, January 28ᵗʰ 1955, that the mercury had dipped well below zero. And during the frenzied rush to the hospital an encounter with an elevated railroad crossing, caused my dad's Buick to take a short but terrifying flight. The following bone jarring landing, prodded me in attempting to catch a premature glimpse of my new surroundings. But thankfully with legs tightly clinched and screaming, my mother was delivered just in time. This was just a preview of my adventures in the years to follow. So, after the usual sharp crack on the bare bottom, I was finally proclaimed healthy and released to begin the wonderful and exciting human stage called childhood.

• • • • •• • • • • ••• ••• • •• •• • •

One of the most essential skills for an aspiring child adventurer to develop is the ability to make planned escapes. After all, nothing diminishes your opportunities for mischief than the actual presence of a parent or an adult. True mischief must be performed in secrecy or at least in the presence of a willing co-conspirator. The first required skill is the art of climbing, of which I was told I had a great natural talent. But to perform a truly legendary feat of mischief, one which would be told around the family circles for years to come, one has to add the unexpected or sensational. Listen, kids have been climbing out their cribs ever since man first designed them, so what would be required which would propel me into the mischief hall of fame, that special ingredient, that icing on the cake, the coup de grace. The infantile idea struck me as suddenly as the disappearance of a babies smile when looked upon by the face of a stranger. I would have to do it bare butt naked.

Picture the scene, a blustery October night, the trees nearly leafless from the onslaught of the autumn's winds, a full moon dressing up the night sky, my dad sleeping peacefully, under the warm covers of a tattered and gaudy colored guilt, his loud and raucous snoring driving my mother to mutter insanities and cuss words only a drunken sailor should utter, When, suddenly, their nighttime bliss is shattered by a loud and insistent knocking at the door. I need to stop and regress a bit here, if you are looking to create a truly unforgettable incident of biblical proportions, you need to remember this axiom, location, location, location. In the realm of driving your parents a little closer to wearing drool bibs and taking up residence at the local padded cell, the axiom for an inspiring child adventurer is timing, timing, timing.

The event must coincide with a specific point on the time line continuum to achieve its greatest potential in removing any sense of rationale and normalcy your parents tentatively cling too. The perfect timing for this escapade was when my parents were snuggled in their bed, where the stresses of the day are being replaced by soft, gentle and safe dreams with the reassurance that the kids are safely tucked into their beds. This is the kind of evil genius that only the really sick can appreciate. Well back to the story, the loud and insistent knocking at the door finally roused my father and after wrapping himself up in a well-worn but gaudy patterned bathrobe, he shuffled, bleary-eyed, towards the kitchen door. Now any time someone is knocking on your door at three in the morning it's a pretty good bet it's not the Readers Digest Sweepstakes Prize patrol.

The person standing at the door was a local police officer and he instantly began to barrage my father, in an accusatory tone, if he had a son about 16 to 18 months of age, ah yes, folks to become proficient and to be able to amply compete with the other rising stars, you need to start young, my dad staring bleary eyed at the inquiring officer responded, "Well officer yes I do", the accusatory tone of the police officer was a nice touch, it provided the necessary emotional tension required for a great drama. The officer fired off the second question, "And where to the best of your knowledge is your son right now", "in bed where I put him" my dad answered tersely, "Well then who the hell does this kid belong too" bellowed the officer. Ah, have you seen the credit card commercials where they unashamedly depict scenes of blatant consumerism and finish off with the word priceless, well the look on my father's face when the police officer pulled my chubby and naked body into my dad's gaze was absolutely priceless. The officer told my dad, in a further accusatory tone, to count his blessings and then scolded him to be more vigilant, he explained that he had found me sitting stark naked in the middle of the intersection and he had missed running me over by a mere few inches. As you can see, planning and executing mischief is like Michelangelo painting the Sisten chapel, or Beethoven writing the 5th symphony, its takes vision and it takes craftsmanship. Unfortunately, unlike Michelangelo or Beethoven, whose reward was money and fame, my parental admiration and reward for this early morning escapade, was a net placed over the top of my crib and an almost constant supply of supervision. Ah, but in the back of my small and somewhat misshapen brain, the seeds of mischief had been planted.

And as my parents whispered words of concern about my behavior, they had failed to recognize the attributes that I possessed which would neutralize their future attempts at minimizing my exploits, I was cute, I was highly motivated and I had plenty of time.

• • •• • • • •

Toddlers have an affinity for copious amounts of curiosity, couple
that with energy levels that would leave the energizer bunny twitching in
the dust and you have two characteristics which can lead to increasing
knowledge and independence but can also lead to a condition called
granulation, the process of physical scarring. Being generously endowed
with both characteristics and a little more than normal air volume
between the ears; I was about to run head long, literally, into my first
encounter with the condition called granulation. Have you ever noticed
that there are basically two types of toddlers, those that listen and those
that don't, "Bobby don't place your hand on that hot stove". "Bobby
don't stick those peas up your nose", "Bobby don't wrestle with the dog
while he's trying to eat". Well, you have probably come to the
conclusion that I was truly the later of the two types, the non-listener.
These children are also placed into other kinds of generalizations such as,
"he never looks before he leaps", God purposely broke the mold when he
made that one", "I worry that he'll make it to three years of age" and
"does brain damage run in the family". I have to ashamedly admit that I
was not the easiest child to rear. Coupled with the fact that my mother
had a tremendous blood phobia, I am surprised she wasn't wearing a
strait jacket as part of her every day wardrobe and popping valium as a
kind of special vitamin supplement. Even to this day when I ask her what
it was like to raise me, her eyes would glaze over and she would begin to
mumble in something akin to speaking in tongues.

I believe all children have a fatal attraction with some creature of the
animal kingdom or an unusual obsession with shiny objects. For
example, my sister Gail could not resist the temptation of sticking her
tongue upon a metal object just recently coated with a fresh covering of
frost, yup you get the picture. But for me, I had a deep unusual obsession
for cows. If you ask me to this day what I found so fascinating with a
bovine mammal which basically just mooed, milked and pooped, I could
not give you a logical answer. Maybe it was their pretty big brown eyes
or that the fact that they came in interesting upholstery patterns, but for
the record, anytime I came near a herd of those cud chewing monsters I
would kick it into over drive just to get a close and personal
observational advantage.

Now you have to understand that most of the facts to this particular
story, being too young to have fully developed a long-term memory,

came from the constant retelling by my father and one of my dad's friends named Gene Verhagen. That day, they had decided to go to a local farm to procure some fencing material and mom, after having just taken one of her special vitamin supplements, pleaded with my father to take me along. Riding in a car on a hot, sunny, summer day was a real pleasure for me. Long before the advent of automobile air conditioning, the only cooling mechanism used in those days is the same method that dogs use today. Hang your head out the car window while drooling incessantly. Besides it was kind of cool to see how far you could stretch that string of salvia hanging out of your mouth before it broke and splattered upon the windshield of the car following to close behind.

But before long, the concrete streets of the city turned into the asphalt roads of the country where images of brightly painted barns of red and white streaked across the back of my retinas, while the freshly manure covered pastures rapidly cleared up any issues with your nasal passages usually faster than an application of Vicks vapor rub.

It was not long before my father turned onto the gravel driveway of a typical Wisconsin dairy farm and parked the car. The loud and raucous barking of the farm dogs as they ran up to the car alerted the farmer to our arrival and it wasn't long before the farmer emerged from the barn and walked over to greet Gene and my father. After explaining to my dad that the dogs were rather harmless and that the blood on their lips wasn't contributed by any humans, to the best of his knowledge, I finally was released from the confines of the car where I then proceeded to follow my dad to the back door of the farmhouse. The smell of freshly brewed coffee, homemade bread and pungent cow manure is to me as wholesome as the feel and smell of finely misted salty sea air is to a sailor.

But it wasn't long and I became quickly bored with the conversation between the adults and I soon wandered onto the back porch of the faded lap sided farmhouse. I was shading my eyes against the powerful rays of the summer sun when I began to scan the barnyard and the green expanse of hay and yellow corn fields; when, what to my wandering eyes should appear but a herd of Holstein cows lazily grazing in a pasture just past the faded barn.

With a sudden explosion of excitement, I leapt off the porch and at break neck speed ran to greet my bovine objects of desire. At the last moment my father had walked out of the back door and instantly became aware of my mad dash and in a flash of horror realized that I had not noticed that between me and my desire were five strands of bristling, sharp barbed wire. My dad started screaming my name and intensely commanding me to stop and as I turned my head towards his direction, I impacted the barbed wire fence. The collision sent me sprawling backwards and in a few seconds my dad had scooped me up into his arms and was sprinting towards the direction of the car. The barbed wire fence had caught me across the face and had opened a large and deep gash across my left cheek. My father placed me into the waiting arms of Gene Verhagen who cradled me and tried to stop the copious amounts of bleeding while my dad drove furiously to get me to our doctor's office. Gene later recounted that he was appalled at the gaping wound which says a lot coming from a combat Navy veteran of the Second World War. And my father stated that I was crying not because I had injured myself but because I had been forced to leave my cud chewing friends behind. The scar on my left cheek is a gentle reminder of my lively childhood and my first introduction into the medical condition called granulation or commonly called scarring.

Over the years it has been, at times, the focal point of initiated conversations and I have to confess of sometimes giving wildly exaggerated explanations. But it was just one of many injuries and adventures that would, over the years, come to change my unmarred dermal landscape and to help forge the person I would later become.

•

• • • •• • • • •• • • •• • •• • • •

After allowing for a sufficient amount of time to pass and finally receiving a pardon from the family warden, I was ready to engage into my next adventure. You would think that after pulling off the first event successfully, the second attempt would be even better and more polished than the first. Yet I have to admit that the second incident teetered on the brink of brainlessness. I guess the vapors of success had left me a little giddy, I was in the beginning phase of social acceptance and I was actually starting to make friends. It wasn't long until I had befriended two other boys of like ages and similar interests. One was Louie Verhagen, my best friend, who lived right next door and Todd VandenBosch, who lived just across the street.

After a hard afternoon of play, which for boys usually consisted of finding the closest dirt pile and then rolling repeatedly around in it, not unlike sun baked hogs trying to cool themselves on a hot august day, or spending hours chasing insects to add to our mason jar collection or lying on the side walk setting up and re-enacting important battles of the Civil War or World War II. I was about to learn a very valuable lesson in the art of mischief, just like the saying that there is no honor among thieves, so goes honor among pursuers of mischief.

Unless you keep a vigilant and suspecting eye upon those people around you, you can become the victim of their pursuit of mischievousness. Back to the beginning, after a hard afternoon of play, Todd had invited me inside of his house for drinks and possibly, to play with his favorite toy; as I learned later in life, this was a ploy to disarm the victim and place them in a much higher state of mischief susceptibility. After allowing me to play with some of his coveted toys, children do have some toys that are more highly valued and prized than others, this again was another ploy to weaken my defenses and to gain my trust, which was an important element in the method of mischief he was about to deploy against me.

After Todd had sufficiently gained my trust, he suddenly told me his mom had said it was time for me to go home, something about any more time spent with me in the house and she would have to obtain a refill of her special vitamins. He then pleasantly walked me to the door and expressed how much he had enjoyed my company, and then without missing a vowel or a consonant, he unleashed the mischief upon me, you have to give him credit because he followed the mischief axiom flawlessly, he proceeded to ask me if I thought it was possible to swallow

[11]

an entire small container of Morton's salt, which he now produced from out of his pocket. After giving this statement extensive intellectual consideration, I said "that little container of salt, I 've seen my dad put more salt than that on his French fries or his popcorn"

It was then that he sprung the hook, the throwing down of the gauntlet, he said " I bet yooooou can't do it", that statement challenges the very core of a boys reputation and courage; so with so much at stake, I conjured up my youthful courage, and with a gleam in my eye and a smirk on my face, I tipped back my head and poured the entire container of salt down the hatch. I'll bet your thinking at this point, man what an idiotic thing to do, painful as it is to admit, this was not one of my best mentally shining moments.

The minute the last grain of salt left the container and began to cascade down my throat, I began to feel the evidence that something resembling disaster was about to strike, imagine someone lost and wandering in the blazing heat of the Sahara Desert and after days of enduring the blast furnace heat of the sun with no water to quench your thirst, your lips dry, cracked and bleeding, the back of your throat constricted and so, so dry. Well, what would take days in the heat of the desert to accomplish, a small container of salt does it in about oooh 10 to 20 seconds. That amount of salt at one time had absorbed every droplet of moisture that my mouth and my throat possessed and then suddenly the walls of my throat suddenly felt constricted and compressed.

As my eyes flew wide open in surprise and fear, I tried to utter words expressing my horror at the subsequent physiological changes but to my dismay not a single syllable could I utter, I had become speechless. Feeling that my small existence upon the earth was about to come to a quick end. I leapt off his porch and with the sounds of Todd's triumphant laughter ringing in my ears, I ran, as if all of the demons of hell were in hot pursuit, with incessant urgency I ran to the one emergency technician that could prevent my premature demise, my mom.

If you are wondering if I had the opportunity or the Moxy for retribution for this wonderful display of masterful mischief, I did. Shortly after my recovery and the taunting of my friends had finally died down, I was once again invited over to Todd's house for some play time. A few days before I had discovered that one of my teeth had become loose. And while over at Todd's home, I discussed this loose tooth with his father, who with great relish confirmed to me that he had the most perfect and painless method of extraction for that loose tooth. He tied one end of the string around the loose tooth and then tied the other end of the string around the door knob of an open door and on the count of three he violently slammed the door shut.

To my surprise the tooth painlessly left my mouth and gracefully arced through the air to land upon the floor of the living room. Todd's father picked up the tooth and with a look of satisfaction, not unlike a surgeon who had just completed a delicate, yet complicated bit of surgery, placed the now extracted tooth into my outstretched hand. Todd and I excitedly examined the tooth, from the white jagged edge of the tooths top to the darkened, bloody root. Now Todd's family had a pet, the breed of the dog escapes me, but it was one of those little yappy kinds of dogs. It also was an aggressive scrounger, if anything resembling food hit the floor, man he was on it faster than a vulture on a road kill.

I don't remember if I even thought about what I was about to do or if it was just a knee jerk reflex based upon my behavioral knowledge of the dog, but as if in slow motion, I launched the tooth out of my hand towards the high-pitched barking dog standing before me. The tooth didn't have time for a second bounce off the living room floor, when the petite canine lunged for it and then swallowed it.

Apparently, the tooth had become lodged in the dog's throat and the dog immediately began retching and gagging and rolling around the floor in a desperate attempt to dislodge the suffocating object. It was as if you ran into a darkened theater with a lit cigar and started screaming fire, Todd's family began to scream and cry and with intense wringing of hands, bewailed upon their father to save the dying family pet. After lifting the dog high into the air and pounding upon the back of the dog, the tooth finally shot out of the dog's mouth. With the dilemma now under control, the previous fear of the family turned to anger and that anger was now directed towards the perpetrator, which of course was me. I was given a sound spanking and then unceremoniously dragged to the front portal of their house, where I was turned out and told never to return again; not unlike an over thrown dictator who had been convicted of crimes against humanity, I was being exiled. At such a young age this type of trauma can be emotionally excruciating, for a day or two, but as it turned out the family moved to Green Bay a little while later that year.

But the experience I learned from Todd's mischievous trick upon me was to become an invaluable lesson.

• •• •• • ••• •• • • •• • • • • • •

I believe that almost every child builds his logical savvy by experiences that are either positive or negative. The ability to thoroughly think through a sequential series of events and to deduce the possible resulting consequences is a matter of trial and error, especially for me. My older sister Gail was the catalyst which helped me to develop this complex cognitive process. I have to admit, in my situation, that my sister Gail had a full year's experience in enhanced logical savvy and with immense pleasure she was willing to provide to me the accelerated, or the Readers Digest condensed version of her lessons. Have you seen, either in personal observation or perhaps while viewing an episode of Wild Kingdom, that certain animals have the distinct ability to pick out the weakest member of the herd and through their heightened sense of smell, they can detect fear itself; well my sister also had some kind of heightened animal ability, she could sniff out an ignorant and gullible individual a full five miles away, not unlike a shark's ability to sense miniscule particles of blood dissolved within the watery vastness of an ocean.

You had to admire my sister's ability to pull the unwary and unsuspecting into her prankster's web, just like card trick artists plying their skills on a busy New York street corner, enticing the wary onlooker with a masterful sleight of hand. Looking back, I wasn't the sharpest tool in the shed, actually, my intellectual quotient was about as sharp as limestone being polished by the continual rush of cold river water, and my sister could smell it.

The day began as any other day for a couple of youngsters, the racing to the cupboard to be the first to lay your hands on the good cereal, just in case it was the last bowl full. You then fill the bowl to just below the overflow level with cereal, and when you are trying to, very carefully, cover the last layer of cereal with milk, your sister reaches out and pushes against my elbow which results in the overflow of milk which is now transforming the table into a scene resembling aerial views of a swollen Mississippi River when it overruns its banks.

After some well-placed backside dusters from my mom and a balanced breakfast of milk, cereal and juice, coupled with some "stop looking at me" remarks and a few MOOOOM, Bob's flinging cereal at me with his spoon again", we were off to the living room for a couple of hours of cartoons. Back in the day, when kids had to walk five miles to

[14]

school through ten-foot snow drifts, both ways, there was very limited television time for cartoons. You had about an hour or two after school, and cartoons from about seven in the morning until noon on Saturdays, unlike the twenty-four-hour cartoon stations of the current era, kids in my time had very little opportunity to be hypnotically baby sat by endless reruns of Sylvester the Cat or Huckle Berry Hound. Which allowed kids of my generation more hours of the day with which to think up imaginative games to play.

My sister who loved to play hide and seek, came up with an imaginative twist to the conventional game of hide and seek, because let's face it, after a couple of days of intensive hiding and seeking, all of the hiding places in the house have been used or had been discovered. She later admitted, that her unusual animal instincts of detecting idiocy had been highly alerted that day, probably because she was able to successfully pull off the what's that on your shirt gag a couple of dozen times that morning, her imaginative twist was to hide from our naturally imprinted authority figure, our mom.

Now it has been scientifically researched that the first-born child in a family has a gene that the rest of the brood doesn't inherit. This gene, which kicks in immediately after the second born child is brought home, provides the first-born child the ability to treat their subordinate siblings with parent-like qualities, mainly taking control and bossing you around. She explained to me that after the exhausting daily drudgeries Mom had to perform, she would probably find this game a breath of fresh air and a respite to her busy work day. Gail also informed me that because Mom's have super powers such as the ability to see you doing things while facing completely in the opposite direction, or to hear you whispering secret information to your siblings from a full room or two away. it became quite obvious that we would have to come up with a new hiding spot, one which we haven't used before, and one which could possibly neutralize Mom's super powers, especially her ability to see through solid objects with the same clarity as Superman. After searching the house for that perfect spot, she suddenly stopped and with a purposeful turn of her head and a smile that resembled that of the wicked witch of the west, she pointed to the place where I would hide, a place that no one had ever used before in a game of hide and seek, a place that would challenge even the most skilled player of hide and seek, the cupboard.

With eager anticipation, usually associated with individuals who are oblivious to inherent dangers or who have a genetic predisposition to disregard consequential risk, I believe it is called brain damage; I listened

[15]

to my sister as she slowly revealed the details of her ingenious plan. I would wedge myself into one of the tiny spaces of the cupboard, while she hid herself in a place that would provide her with a good view, which she explained was necessary for an accurate and a full recounting of the event for future prosperity and fame. After I had pushed the lemon-colored chair across the kitchen floor, I pulled myself up onto the counter top and wedged my small but somewhat pudgy frame into the confining space, I closed the cupboard door and stated that I was ready to play. Now have you ever heard the phrase, "Now I know why they eat their young". It is usually used when in direct contact with an incredible example of idiocy. I had fallen hook line and sinker for the wily whims of my sister.

Picture this, there I am curled up in a small space like a wild fox in a winter's den, with the broken pieces of cups and plates littering the counter top, in a cupboard that has GLASS doors. I was as inconspicuous as the wart on a witch's nose. The look on my mom's face when she surveyed the damaged dishware, and saw my snot nose pressed up against the glass, a face not unlike the look you see on a person when they come across their neighbors two-hundred-pound St. Bernard violating their prize flower bed, was terrifying. After the spanking and the lecture, I threw myself upon my bed and pondered the events of the day, small seeds of logic were beginning to sprout. probably because of the pounds of dirt that had dried behind my ears, that logic was telling me that I would not allow my sister to gain the advantage again with which to feed her diabolical sense of humor or so I said.

Remember small seeds take a while to grow into plants of maturity and I was no exception.

• • • •• •• •

Back in the day, before the advent of electronic home gaming, outdoor activity was the method of play and recreation for kids. And as gaining one's driver license depicts a milestone in maturity and freedom to a teenager, the acquisition of a two wheeled bike marks an important stage in childhood, especially in the areas of transportation and social status. This monumental benchmark would have been perfect except for one little hitch; I had to share that bike with my older sister Gail.

The day my father brought home that 16-inch red bicycle was one of the happiest days for me. It was beautiful with its highly glossed red paint, trimmed out with its dazzling chromed rims and spokes. My sister says the bike was actually dingy red with rust tainted rims and spokes, but that difference in observation did not really matter to me, whatever the condition that bike was in, for me, represented a little piece of sidewalk freedom. Almost immediately, I felt the desire to mount that new metallic steed and ride off into the colorfully tinged sunset. But before those smoky wisps of thoughts had the opportunity to dissipate, my sister Gail had quickly climbed aboard that iron steed and with a sneering, smug smile of triumph, she was gliding it down the grey stained concrete sidewalk.

Sitting slumped over and feeling rather defeated and emotionally jilted, I could feel the tears of disappointment beginning to well up and puddle warmly into the corners of my red streaked eyes. When all of a sudden that tiny little voice, you know that character, that one dressed all in black, sporting a set of forehead horns and carrying a sharply pointed spear, began to speak inside of my head, at first it was faint and barely audible, but as I began to listen more attentively, it suddenly grew louder and more distinct. It's that little voice you always hear just before you get yourself into big trouble. "Come on Bob don't let her get away with this. Do you think the likes of Roy Rodgers or GI Joe would sit here crying like a girl and feeling sorry for themselves or would they take charge and change the course of the ensuing battle. In an instant, a new fuzzy feeling began to course through the sinews of my body. It's that kind of feeling usually reserved for the handsome and courageous hero in a Hollywood classic, who after having been severely beaten and humiliated by the movie villain, and then when all hope is seemly lost, reaches into his bulging pocket and pulls out his last chance, that slightly dented but vitamin packed can of spinach, thanks Popeye. That emerging new feeling quickly turned into a new plan of aggressive action. A plan that would literally save the day, that would rescue the damsel in distress and that would result in the return of my prized stallion. Now that I had a successfully thought up a plan, it was now time to put that brilliant plan into action.

There are usually two courses of action under taken by the movie hero one, to gain the upper hand over his arch rival, either by the direct, damn the torpedoes approach or two, to sneak into the corral, then in a painful cramping crouch, waddle through the stable of horses using them as cover and then when the coast was clear, run hellbent for the back of the barn which would put you into a position that would completely surprise and overwhelm your adversary.

After a moment of careful and reckless deliberation, I chose the last method. Now seeing that my sister Gail was riding continuous laps around the block and could at any moment change her intended direction in which to ride those laps, it became apparent that my approach had to be foolproof. Any lapse in concentration or thoughtless planning would result in a premature discovery and the complete and utter failure of the mission. With the stealth of an experienced female lion approaching her unsuspecting prey, I moved into the predestined ambush location. Sitting silently and still behind the tree that grew in a tilted angle towards the grey stained sidewalk, I waited for the perfect moment in which to spring the insidious trap and regain my esteemed possession, my glorious dingy red, chromed stallion.

The irritating metallic screeching of the bicycle chain rubbing against the guard brought my already tense nervous system to a higher state of alert. The increasing sound of worn rubber tires trying frantically to maintain frictional cohesion, telegraphed that my sister was moving steadily closer. I am told that in the critical moments just prior to engaging in dangerous situations, that the relativity properties of time kick in and time actually slows down. Allowing the individual to relive all of his or her memories in a vivid and rapid pictorial display. Seeing that I was only about 7 years of age, that life flash lasted about 1 millionth of second. As my sister Gail turned the corner of the sidewalk and then proceeded towards my ambush position, my body instinctively assumed a crouched posture. My mouth suddenly felt void of any moisture and my muscles were quivering with the adrenaline rush of excitement. The moment of truth had arrived, my sister, unaware, had approached the unsuspected trap.

With the agility and daring of a young Indian brave, I quickly sprang forward from the side of the tree and in mid-flight, collided with my sister knocking her completely off the bike. Regaining an upright standing position with the athletic skills of a trained gymnast, I ran to the unoccupied bicycle, mounted it, and then pedaled a hasty escape down the street.

For a brief period of time all seemed right with the world, the sun blazed brighter, the air felt crisper and the wind blew warmly yet gently across my face. And best of all, I had regained my metallic steed from the terrible grasp of my arch rival.

There are relationships between man and machine that when engaged in the pursuit of its purpose, that the two blended into one perfect union of motion. Riding away from the decreasing volume of curses and the "I 'm telling mom", cascading from the mouth of my sister Gail, I could feel that perfect blend between my bike and myself. The blocks of concrete sidewalks fell away effortlessly, as the chromed rimmed wheels guided me along. The bike responded to my every command with such smooth precision as if it were reading my intentions just milliseconds prior to their execution, the bike and I had become one.

Yah, I know what you're thinking, every dog has his day, don't do the crime if you can't do the time. Trust me, in a 7-year-olds world justice often comes swiftly and without legal representation.

The life of a fugitive is hard and unnerving. The constant moving from place to place to protect your identity, enduring the harsh elements of mother nature instead of enjoying the warm comforts of an established and well stocked homestead, coupled with the persistent feeling of paranoia that the next person you meet is the one to turn you into the long arm of the law. All of these hardships can quickly turn a strong willed and healthy person to a nail biting, hand wringing, skeleton of his or her former self. The fact that my last nourishing meal was about 4 hours ago and it was about to get dark, I came to the quick realization that my time running from the law, my mom, had come to an end. Turning my handle bar reins towards home, I spurred the pedals of my iron horse and steeled myself for the reaction of the unruly posse waiting for me at home.

Turning the corner at the bottom of the street, I could see the aging but sturdy structure I called home. And to my surprise instead of seeing the brightly lit torches of an inpatient mob, the area was strangely deserted. Could it be that instead of the hanging for bike rustling that I was expecting, I had garnished a reprieve and that my deed had gone unnoticed by the local sheriff. With a renewed sense of hope, I placed my steed into its freshly cleaned stall and headed for the house.

I entered the ponderosa from the back door which opens into a small and musty smelling room that leads to the kitchen or the food cellar. Breaking into a whistle, I walked through my bedroom that I shared with my sister Gail along with the washer and dryer. Upon entering the kitchen to get to the living room, where I was hoping to catch the next episode of the Scare Crow, is where all hell broke loose. It seems that instead of a posse milling about outside, the sheriff had sent the local vigilantes, grumbling back to their homes. She decided that the large torch carrying crowd might have given away her intentions of capture and possibly have scared me away to another unknown location, presumably, my grandparents who lived just a block away.

With the quickness and agility most young mothers possess, she was on me faster than a carb starved dieter on a pile of freshly baked pancakes. In a child's world you can forget the old cliché, innocent until proven guilty or the right to have an attorney present when questioned. Well before I could utter a syllable in my defense, my mother had placed an iron grip upon my left wrist and the spanking quickly ensued, robustly cheered on by the plaintiff, my sister Gail, yelling something like "get him ma, get him". After receiving that disciplinary action, I was place into my room to think about the unacceptable behavior I had bestowed upon my sister earlier that day. Now kids, being sent to your room back in those days was truly punishment, unlike the kids today whose rooms are stuffed with the latest and greatest electronic games and gadgets, our rooms were electronically Spartan in comparison. You were lucky to have maybe a comic book or two, a couple of toys or if you were old enough, possibly a transistor radio to entertain yourself with. Now I am not complaining, looking back, almost all of the spankings I received were truly deserved.

And I believe kids today are not disciplined enough. But it beats the alternative, back in the days when cowboys ruled the west, and where rustlers and horse thieves were actually hanged for their crimes.

• • • •• • • • ••

Thor, the Norse god of war was the son of the chief god called Odin. A creature of mythology that was transformed into a comic book character whose adventures mesmerized the imaginations of many a small lad and all of that glorious adventure was available at the local corner grocery for about twenty-five cents an issue. All super heroes possessed some kind of non-natural power that enabled them to successfully engage their arch rivals and then against all odds, defeat them thus saving the world, our local communities and the occasional lovely damsel in distress. And the mythical creature named Thor had a specially powered weapon, that weapon was the hammer of Odin.

I remember, to the best of my aging memory, that it was the fourth of July and it had all of the signs of being a scorcher. My parents were up early and were busily preparing the backyard for a fourth of July party that they were hosting. Being a parent of four children, I understand that these types of situations, with your attention focused elsewhere, can provide a window of opportunity for disaster and possible injury and trust me; disaster was lurking just around the corner. If you have ever viewed television episodes of Dennis the Menace you have a pretty good picture of what it was like being my parents. Dennis wasn't a mean kid, just a boy with a lot of passionate energy who lacked the ability to look before he leapt or understood the concept of consequences or possibly having both oars in the water. Even though his intentions were always good, his lack of fore sight always ended up causing agitation for his parents and of course his neighbors the Wilson's. It was rumored that Dennis's character profile was modeled after me and after looking back I am inclined to believe it was true.

After having completed the routine nuisances of teasing my sister Gail and pestering my parents with the usual "whatcha ya doing", coupled with a thousand "but why's", I sauntered over to my friend Louie's house to see if he could come out and play. I always loved going over to Louie's house. His mother made homemade bread, I don't mean occasionally made homemade bread, no, she made homemade bread every week. That house was always filled with the mouthwatering, sumptuous smell of freshly baked bread and it always tasted as wonderful as it smelled. I can't quite remember what we did for those few morning hours in Louie's house, but I do remember the moment we decided to engage in the activity that would leave me a permanent scar and ruin my parents carefully planned Fourth of July party.

Most kids are inherently born with a huge reservoir of curiosity and they spend a good portion of their time examining the many new and exciting aspects of their environment. Give any kid an empty mason jar and he'll come home with the jar filled with various species of insects and if the critter is too big to fit inside the clear confines of the mason jar, his jean pockets will do just fine. Hey, if it wasn't for the rambunctious nature of boys to roll around in every conceivable type of dirt known to man, detergent companies would never have had the opportunity to develop the phrase "New and Improved".

I do remember we were on the corner of our street and we had noticed a line of ants marching towards and away from a crack in the sidewalk. With our curiosity meter pegged into the danger zone, we got down upon our young and knobby knees and observed their curious activity. With the discipline of a well-trained military force, they were marching in perfect columnar order and I could swear I heard them singing in a barely audible but high pitch voice, "your left, your left, your left right left, damn it private antsy get in step with the rest of the company, what's the matter with you boy, born with eight left feet. Company halt, half right huh", anybody with military training will understand what comes after that last command and it sure isn't purty.

After a brief span of awed observation, remember the attention span of a seven-year-old boy is about 20 nano seconds, our youthful imaginations kicked into high gear. Suddenly, they were not just a line of ants scouring the countryside. They became an army; an army of ants bent upon the destruction of human kind. In the mind's eye of imagination, they became evil, ugly creatures, devoid of any compassion or mercy. Just hell bent to impose their single-minded purpose upon us, and then to ultimately rule the rest of the free world. It suddenly became our duty to save that world from such an evil and corrupt intent. It was time to shed our disguises of your normal, run of the mill, seven-year-old appearances and expose our true identities, young snot nosed super heroes.

We leapt into action, sprinting to our homes to gain possession of our treasured weapon, the hammer of Thor, a weapon no enemy could withstand. Now my dad had two hammers, one had the normal bent claws with which one removed nails and the other hammer had straight back claws. Now give a seven-year-old boy a choice, he will usually choice the one that presents the most danger to himself. You guessed it, I chose the hammer with the straight back claws.

Upon returning to the battleground, we proceeded to wade into our enemy's ranks without concern for our own safety, we fought the creatures bravely and with relentless ferocity. At first it seemed that the tide of battle was ours, but for every enemy we vanquished, a dozen would take its place. As I raised my hammer even higher to deliver a more devastating stroke, I felt a blow at the back of my head. Momentarily stunned, I wavered and then with renewed vigor delivered the strike against the enemy. I could see we were now getting the upper hand against our foes which seemed to be retreating back into their dark underground fortress.

With all of the energy I had left I raised Thor's mighty hammer over my head to deliver the last deciding blow and then proceeded to sink the claws of the hammer into the soft blood filled back of my cranium. With a painful tug I removed the hammer and looked to my band of brother companion Louie and asked if I was bleeding. I could tell by the stunned, frightened look upon his face that I indeed was wounded. I placed my hand to the back of my head and when I looked at the palm of my hand, it was covered in blood. It is amazing how blood can quickly transform an imaginative, immortal super hero back into a mere seven-year-old boy.

With a blood curdling scream I took off running to find the only people who could save me from my fateful wound, my parents. Now imagine a seven-year-old boy screaming and crying at the loudest setting his lungs could muster. A boy with blood smeared all over his face and head running through the joyous throng of friends, family and neighbors who had gathered in his backyard to celebrate the fourth of July with his parents. Imagine this boy not just running to the safety of his parents, but continued to run laps around those fine folks screaming and bleeding and begging God to spare the life of such a young and delicate soul. The ladies began to scream and cry, while the men began running, desperately, trying to catch me, not unlike the event at the state fair of trying to catch the greased pig. The emotional state of the party went from a joyous holiday celebration to a somber state akin to being a witness to a plane crash. I was finally collared and brought to the local doctor's office for a round of suturing. I was brought home and put to bed to recover from my battlefield injury. And Thor's hammer was placed back into a secret location known only by one of the greater gods, my father.

[23]

But you know what they say, you can never keep a good super hero down and besides, the horizon of future adventures stretched before me like the glittering surface of the Pacific Ocean. It was really, only just merely a matter of time.

· · · ·· · · · ·· ·

I remember the day when I learned what the word hot really meant. As a young child, I had the habit of staring mesmerized at the stove, as the scratched and discolored circular iron bars would turn from a dull boring red to a bright interesting orange in color. My mother would always give me the same warning, "Bob don't touch, that's gonna be hot." Now I know what you're thinking, but hey what do you expect from a child who was given a name that can be spelled correctly either forward or backwards. So, one fateful day, after my mom gave me the usual warning, I found that I could no longer resist the temptation. With eyes wide open in excited expectation, I placed my young, scar free hand upon the beautiful, glowing, orange iron coils. That was the day I learned that hot is associated with excruciating pain accompanied by loud screams and large blisters. What I was about to now learn was what the word beehive meant.

Growing up in the early sixties, many people still grew and tended vegetable rich gardens in their backyards, even in the city where lots were rather small. I guess it was a holdover from living during the depression when jobs and food was plenty scarce. I remember the stories that my grandparents would regale of their Spartan existence during those lean years. That for weeks at a time they lived on popcorn and potato flavored water; unfortunately for them, macaroni and cheese still hadn't yet been invented and then having to walk along the cities railroad tracks searching for pieces of coal, with which was used to feebly heat their house and at the same time avoiding the railroads enforcer whose job it was to prevent such theft of railroad property. Now I understand that whenever I would ask grandpa to make some popcorn why his eyes would suddenly glaze over and he would begin to mutter to himself incomprehensibly as if he were reliving some catastrophic event. So, gardens back then were kind of an insurance policy against starvation just in case the stock market ever decided to take another calamitous nose dive. Besides, those gardens were also a great repository of vegetable weaponry that we used to redecorate the sides of unsuspecting cars or non-participating houses on those dark and blustery Halloween nights.

Okay, association is a marvelous and powerful tool in the learning process. Think about it, we learn a word's meaning through association. You point to a car or a tree or a dog, say the word and the child learns what that object is associated with. But associative learning also has its downside. As children, we are constantly bombarded with stories and cartoons utilizing animals. But these animals are given human characteristics with which to convey the story line. For example, in the story the Jungle Book, the wise old bear Baloo is given a warm, caring, friendly personality. How many visitors to Yellow Stone National Park have been bitten or mauled by bears because of their unrealistic knowledge of bear behavior. "Hey honey doesn't that bear look just like Baloo." "Oh, how cute." "Can you take a picture of me giving Baloo a great big bear hug". Not only animals such as bears but insects are also conveyed to children as having human characteristics, Bee-good, Bee-nice, Bee all that you can bee in the Army, sorry I got a little carried away. Well anyway you get the point. Because of those associations, children and adults are imprinted with false impressions concerning animals or insects which results in our natural defense mechanisms becoming dulled and useless. So, when the kindly apron wearing elderly woman gave my sister and I the warning to watch out for the beehive located somewhere in her garden and now because of our dulled defense mechanisms concerning such critters, we did not give enough credence to her worthy warning. But Mother Nature was about to give us a reality check, her classroom was soon to be in session.

I recall that it was a really beautiful late summer day in Wisconsin and I had just rolled my sister Gail off me, who had been pummeling me for torturing her Barbie dolls, hey I was playing GI Joe and I was just trying to extract some information from Barbie about the location of suspected enemy insurgents, when suddenly mom informed us that we were going up the street to pick some blackberries. Now there were only a few statements in my youth that would capture my entire attention, "remember Bob, tomorrow we have to go the doctor and get your immunization shots" or "get ready were going to pick some blackberries". There were two things that I loved to pick from the vine, peas and blackberries. The usual method of picking blackberries was eat one, store one, eat two, store one, eat three, store one, well you get the idea. With a gleam in my eye and my salivary glands running overtime, we proceeded up the alley to the blackberry patch located just two blocks away.

Upon arrival, my sister and I were given a pint basket to place the picked blackberries into and soon we were engaged in picking, eating and storing. After satisfying our gluttonous demand for blackberries and filling only about one of the pint baskets, my sister and I decided it was time to play. And the game we picked to play was tag.

It was the perfect environment to play the game tag. With all of the different rows of vegetables and blackberry vines you had a much easier time in evading your pursuer. The initial trepidation about the beehive was now growing dim with the exuberant nature of our play. I had just turned the corner of a row, chasing my sister, when I saw her suddenly stop and throw her arms up over her head. I thought she was giving up to my superior gaming ability and I turned on the after burners to place the anticipated tag upon her. But instead, what I ran into was not a display of surrender but a huge swarm of really angry hornets.

My sister had stepped upon the large beehive that was burrowed into the soft turned up ground beneath her feet. I can recall the sudden onslaught of the hornets as they converged upon our heads, our necks, our backs and our legs. My sister and I were attempting to stand our ground and we were trying frantically to defend ourselves by uselessly waving our arms over our heads and then forcibly brushing our heads and necks trying desperately to dislodge those painful stinging insects. At first, our defense was done silently but soon the intensifying pain from the attack purged the air from our lungs in ear shattering screams.

My mom suddenly realizing our tormented situation, ran down the row and without missing a step, scooped us up, one under each arm and continued to run towards home. I then remember being in doctor Cherkasky's office and receiving shots to combat the pain and immense swelling I was experiencing. And the next few days the window to my world was much smaller due to the small painful slits formed by my bee stung swollen eyelids. My sister and I had been stung about 30 to 40 times and escaped death only because of the brave actions of our mother and the expertise of our family doctor.

But Mother Nature taught us the real meaning of the word BEEHIVE and from that time on, whenever I saw or heard of a beehive, I made sure I placed as much distance as possible between those painful stingers and myself.

• • • •• • • • •• • •• • • • •

When I was a kid, Saturday mornings were the best time for televised adventure. From cartoons to cowboy westerns, Saturday morning was the one time slot designed especially for kids. And one of my favorite shows was Roy Rodgers. No matter how dastardly the villains or if Roy was out numbered twenty to one, you could count on that cowboy with the twin pearl handled six shooters to win the day, to save the town and to win the girl of his fancy. Not only was Roy the best shot, the best roper, the best fighter and the best looking, he could also pull out his trusty six stringed guitar and belt out a pretty good western tune. Now you could conceivably argue that other western legends were better than ole Roy: he did not have the steely eyed, grimed face nature of Clint Eastwood or the heavily laden testosterone swagger of John Wayne or the suave sophistication of Brett Maverick, but none of those western superheroes, after perpetrating justice upon the villainous outlaws, could gaze into the eyes of the prettiest cowgirl in town and melt her heart with a stirring rendition of Home, Home on the Range.

Besides, what's the point in placing your life in jeopardy and your reputation on the line for just mere honor and glory, when you could be rewarded with something much more satisfying such as respect and romance. Now it's easy to discuss western movie complexity when your fifty-three years old, but back then, the part of the Roy Rodgers show that really put a twinkling gleam in my eye was his beautiful golden-haired partner, his horse named Trigger.

As a wild-eyed gun slinging eight-year-old kid, I had all the necessary components required to become a successful western hero except for one important ingredient, a horse. It's kind of hard to leave a lasting impression upon the good citizens of town, when after defeating the evil villain and his despicable cronies, was to walk away into the sunset wearing your high-top sneakers.

I just had to obtain a horse and at my tender age, the ability to create any kind of wealth was pretty limited, I was too young to operate a lawn mower, I was too young to get a paper route, hell I was too young to even understand the concept of bottle deposits. For you more recent generations, I grew up in the age of milk delivery, transistor radios, vinyl records and the hula hoop. Soda in cans was still just a gleam in some marketer's eye. Soda back then was sold in bottles and when you returned the empty bottle to the store, they gave you a shiny new dime.

[28]

That bottle deposit was to encourage consumers to return the empty bottles so the soda manufacturers could promptly refill them. Well anyway, I was left rather hopeless as an entrepreneur. I had only one option available to me, to forsake my current rambunctious life style and to place my dreams of getting a horse into the only person I knew that could fulfill such an ambitious request, that individual was the one and only, cookie eating, milk guzzling jolly old elf, Santa Claus. I immediately sat down and in my best Crayola handwriting pleaded my case to the big jolly old elf.

For the next few months my mother was rather perplexed over the change in my behavior. At first, she thought I had come down with some strange malady, treated by repeated doses of Castor Oil, but after a trip to the doctor's office and a week-long session with the local exorcist, my change in behavior was finally accepted as genuine. And now the wait for Christmas day was becoming the longest and most grueling time of my young and tender life. Not to mention the emotional and psychological trauma I had to endure in allowing the plethora of sister pestering opportunities I had to let pass by, unchallenged.

But finally, old man time turned the calendar page to Christmas Eve and I began to overflow with excitement. I could barely sleep a wink that night, tossing back and forth between periods of great anticipation which suddenly turned into periods of anguishing disappointment. Was I good enough this year, did I leave enough milk and cookies for Old Saint Nick and his reindeer? At this juncture it had become a moot point,

Christmas Eve had arrived, tomorrow, Christmas Day, would end any speculation and as I slowly drifted off into the realm of sleep, visions of prancing horses danced through my head, at least one blonde plastic replica.

As I awoke on Christmas morning, two distinct sensory experiences greeted my rising, the artistic color of crimson spread across dawn's horizon and the sound of rats running to and fro inside the walls of my bedroom.

With a shout of glee, I jumped from my bed, barely missing the devastating right cross my sister had tried to deliver for waking her up so early, and bounded for the living room.

As I turned the corner of the hallway and entered the living room, the glare of the multi colored lights and the gleam of the highly polished ornaments was almost blinding. My dad, a self-taught electrician, took great pride in calculating how many tree lights he could arrange upon the evergreen tree without exceeding the limits of ozone or possibly reaching the Christmas tree's flash point. I began too eagerly scan the brightly lit room for the form of my Christmas passion, but to my great disappointment, no evidence was to be seen. My disappointment soon turned into anger, I could not believe that that crimson costumed, trimmed in white, overweight elf had stiffed me. Especially, after I had worked so hard to abandon my typical Dennis the Menace behavioral traits; couple with the fact that my older sister Gail had gotten off so easily the last six months. Hell, I was on the road to potential sainthood. Emotionally dejected, I sat down on the living room couch and waited for the rest of the family to arrive.

It was rather painful to watch the joy of my fellow siblings, squealing with glee, as they opened their colorful and neatly wrapped overabundance of Christmas gifts. Shards of twinkling wrapping paper filled the air as they bore into their newly found treasures like a pack of wolves at a fresh kill site. I began opening my presents with the emotional level akin to a death row inmate reading his Governor's reasoning for not staying his execution.

When suddenly my mother interrupted me and asked me what was wrong, I then broke into tears and between sobs I tried to explained to my mom how disappointed I was with not having received the one gift I had so desperately wanted. Expecting the usual Ward Clever to Beaver speech about how life is not always fair and to be thankful for what I did have, I was surprised when my dad announced that he had discovered a misplaced present in the foyer by the front door.

Leaping off my mom's lap, I bounded across the living room and slid to a stop upon the well-worn and stained hard wood floor, I came face to face with the reality of my yuletide dream. There standing upon its finely sanded and stained oak supports, was the most beautiful plastic stallion I had ever trained my red rimmed and tear-stained eyes upon. It was the exact duplicate of Trigger, the wonderful, brave and well-trained steed of my favorite western hero. Its vibrant blonde body was trimmed with a brilliant white mane and tail. Without hesitation, I jumped into the saddle and grabbed the reins, I then rode off into my first imaginary western adventure.

Well, you can pretty well imagine that was the turning point of any of my future western escapades. There wasn't a villain villainous enough, a gang tough enough to withstand the judicial virtues and bravery of my steed and myself. The notches on the pistol grip of my chromed side firearms were rapidly growing and my reputation was quickly spreading across the vast fruited plains and the snow-capped mountains of the west.

I was living the most satisfying imaginative time of my youth, life was good and the future only promised still more successful and rewarding western campaigns,

That is, until a cloudy and rainy spring day brought it all to a grim and screeching halt. I awoke that morning, gulped down my breakfast, grappled with my sister and ran to tend to the needs of my plastic stallion. After being rebuked by my mother for yet another episode of sleep walking and urinating into the kitchen garbage can, I quickly donned my western garb and headed to the sheriff's office to determine what western hero action was needed for this particular day. Maybe to foil a gang of cattle rustlers or to battle a land baron wanting to unlawfully acquire a neighbor's ranch or possibly to interrupt a well-planned bank robbery or possibly to see if the villains were merely taking a needed day off to lick their wounds acquired by yours truly. If no other dastardly deeds were on the day's docket, there were always some hostile Indians that needed to be headed off.

After a couple of cups of strong brewed black coffee, the sheriff informed me that the Hartjes gang, that was a group of rather rough boys who lived across the alley, was planning to rob the stage coach of its gold shipment. With a gleam in my eye, I proceeded down the weather worn planks of the town's sidewalk, while greeting the kindly women folk with a tip of my hat and then I headed towards the stable that stalled my trusty steed.

As I entered the dusty but dry stable, I was greeted with a loud and excited whiney from my faithful companion. Stepping into the plastic formed stirrup and placing my hand upon the smooth and shiny saddle horn, I nimbly boosted myself upon her strong, golden back and with a high, ho Silver, I know that's from a different cowboy show but damn it sure sounds good, out of town I rode. Leaving a cloud of dry dust stubbornly suspended in midair. My intentions were to rendezvous with the gold laden stage coach and the treacherous Hartjes gang just prior to the robbery. Knowing that the perfect ambush point was a spot on the trail about ten miles west of town, a place where the road dipped steeply down and the ragged boulders of the landscape jutted awkwardly skyward, I spurred my four-legged companion into an even faster gait in an attempt to reach the ambush point in time to spoil the gang's villainous plan.

With a slight inward pressure of my knees and a loud, raspy he-ya, my steed sprang quickly into high gear. The sudden acceleration nearly catapulted me backwards and off my mount, but with a steely resolve I leaned forward into the saddle and with the wind now pushing the front of my cowboy hat flat against the felt top, we sprinted across the arid and dusty landscape. Upon arriving at a spot just behind and slightly above the suspected ambush location, I tied the reins of my horse to a nearby cactus and crawled to the top of a rock outcropping to get a better view. Sure enough, down below me was the Hartjes gang, crouched in a tight circle.

It looked like the leader was drawing out the details of their criminal scheme in the sand. When suddenly the sound of the stage coach could be heard approaching the final bend in the road. The Hartjes gang sprang to life, some members of the gang, in a crouched fashion, hastened to their pre-planned ambush locations, while the remaining members of the gang ran to a large boulder. And with the aid of huge tree limb, broke loose the boulder from its stationary bed and sent it crashing down onto the roadway below. In an instant, I knew how the Hartjes gang was going to stop the stage coach and steal the precious baggage of gold.

I also knew that when the stage coach came to a stop in front of the boulder, the driver and the man riding shotgun would become easy targets for the hiding members of the criminal gang. I had to act and act quickly if I wanted to save the lives of the two stage coach employees.

With the agility and quickness of a cheetah, I sprang from my vantage point and raced towards the bottom ledge of the rock outcropping. Stopping at the edge of the precipice, I gave out a sharp, high-pitched whistle. My trusty horse, whinnying in return, dashed to below my precarious position and with the iron nerves of a stunt pilot or the bad judgment of a drunken sailor, I leapt off the boulder and landed directly into the curved, hard shape of my plastic saddle. Thank God, that at eight years of age, one does not have to worry about permanently damaging the ole family jewels.

Now folks, it was at this most critical moment in my imaginary play that the whole scene quickly went to hell in a hand basket. Being a western hero and constantly dealing with the ill-tempered outlaws of the day, one has to project oneself to the public, at least, with a kind of rough and raw vitality. Winking at the pretty ladies and occasionally spitting bubble gum juice great distances is considered to be socially acceptable, but cussing, especially cussing at such a tender young age, brings out the quick and sure wrath of God, who was telepathically linked to my mother the executioner of God's quick and sure wrath. I recall the words that invoked a punishment so swift and severe that for weeks a rumor was circulated that I was actually dead and not on a scheduled Disney vacation.

Upon landing into the saddle of my steed, I hollered, "Giddy up you son of a bitch, we've got some fucking outlaws to round up". The hand of God, played by my mother, yanked me swiftly from my plastic equestrian and delivered a vicious spanking while sputtering unintelligible syllables and incomplete sentences.

After expending her angry energy into the round and now somewhat numb backside of my Levi jeans, she proceeded to pull me into the bathroom for the second part of my three-part punishment.

This portion of the punishment consisted of placing a bar of soap into my mouth and a lecture on the severe case of my verbal misjudgment. The third portion of my punishment consisted of a two-week grounding in lieu of a mandatory jail sentence, thus forming the seed for the rumor of my untimely demise.

After a two-week grounding, I didn't visit nor play with my rocking horse for a while. It wasn't that I had suddenly lost any affection for my trusty steed but instead I had turned my attention to the gathering threat towards our allied nations from the countries of Germany and Japan. It was time to put a stop to the blitzkrieg advance of the Nazi army and to the island gobbling invasions of the Imperial Japanese militia.

Besides, a great imagination requires a key ingredient and that key ingredient is variety. And I was ready to immerse myself in its adventurous lather.

• • • •• • ••

There has always been a great debate amongst people whether incidents that happen in one's life is by way of fate, coincidence or divine providence. I am going to propose another theory, the theory of just plain stupidity. Oh, I believe there are those unexplainable events that if one ponders long enough, one could arrive at a conclusion that would give credence to fate, coincidence or divine providence or perhaps a trip to their local physician in search of a brain tumor caused by such a long and intense pondering. For example, a train leaves the railway station at exactly one thirty pm traveling at a speed of fifty miles per hour. At the exact same time, a rusted, lime, green station wagon is backing out of the driveway on his way to Bubba's farm. Hey, it's cheaper than taking your kids to the fee-based petting zoo or the time and expense required to visit a real zoo.

Anyway, at the same time, grandma decided to take her little fluffy, a yapping ankle biter pooch, for a walk down the quiet, lonely back road near her residence. As the station wagon is approaching the railroad tracks, the kids in the back seat are engaged in their favorite activity, which is driving the driver of said vehicle absolutely nuts and dangerously distracted. Anyone with children can identify with this situation, "Dad she's staring at me again", "dad he's touching me". "Caroline stop staring at your brother", "Brad Please stop touching your sister and no we are not there yet".

As the car approaches the rail road crossing, the driver, peering almost constantly into the rear-view mirror to monitor his children's next shenanigans is unaware of the iron locomotive bearing down on said intersection.

Meanwhile grandma is rapidly approaching the same intersection in the opposite direction, in grandma terms, the definition of rapidly is somewhere near the speed of smell. When suddenly, the driver of the station wagon see's the speeding train out of the corner of his eye and that's when time begins to utilize Einstein's theory of relativity, where time actually slows down. In cinematic perfect slow motion, the driver of the car, in milliseconds, responds by mashing down on the accelerator, the train's engineer upon seeing that the station wagon is not going to stop in time, applies his powerful hydraulic brakes. Meanwhile grandma is totally unaware of the rapidly developing catastrophe, her attention is diverted away from the dangerous scene because fluffy is laying his fifth yard mine on her neighbor's front yard.

The accelerating car crosses the raised rail road tracks with mere inches to spare from being T-boned by the three-hundred-ton, spark eschewing, behemoth. The car is now airborne and when it finally comes back to rest upon the glossy, black asphalt road, the worn-out shocks cause the car to violently fish tail which then causes the driver to lose control and wham, grandma and the pooch are suddenly vaporized. The only recognizable remnants are grandma's bent and twisted walker and little fluffy's diamond encrusted collar.

Now was this caused by fate, destiny or divine intervention? The mathematics involved in trying to solve all the variables that lead up to this tragedy is mind blowing. If the train had left the station just ten seconds later, or if dad had properly tranquilized his children prior to departure, or if grandma had gotten her needed cataract surgery and had replaced the batteries in her hearing aids. If any one of these variables had changed, the accident, conceivably, would not have happened.

Now the theory of stupidity is different from the complex example just given. The theory of stupidity is different in two ways, it does not require complex math and it does not require a myriad of variables.

Now stupidity has just two main ingredients, a lower than standard IQ quotient and the inability to have more than one thought at a time.

Most mentally sufficient children, being placed in a potentially harmful circumstance, would stop and consider the consequence of their actions. However, some of us were born without that proper sequence of amino acid chaining and that deficiency was about to reach up and slap me in the face or more correctly, the eye.

I had spent the day hiding out from my older sister. It seems that first born children inherit a subordinate parent gene. This allows them to boss and intimidate their younger siblings just as if they were an actual parent. Fortunately, the gene is only activated when the actual parent is not within sight or earshot.

There were days when my mom was absolutely frantic about why I was sweat soaked and unceremoniously clamped to one of her ankles where she had to laboriously drag me around the house while attempting to finish her chores. Unbeknown to my mother, those hours spent being dragged around the house was as refreshing as a workaholic executive being able to play a round of relaxing golf, especially when my sister's parental gene was having a rather intense flare up.

[35]

I remember I was curled up, like a contortionist, and hiding from my sister in the kitchen garbage can when I heard a knock on the door. I immediately began to rock the garbage can until it rolled over and I was able to pour myself out and answer the door.

It was one of my best friends, Jerry VanDynHoven, he stayed and we played outside for a while doing what boys did back in those days, running, climbing trees, playing army, chasing each other, collecting bugs or rolling around in the dirt.

It was a glorious time to grow up, unlike children of today, where they wake up and spend hours gazing at the brilliant phosphorus computer or television screens while following pre-programmed mazes or situations. When we would wake up, we would wake up with the soft glow of the rising sun, our fresh imaginations churning with the anticipation of what the new day would bring.

After a quick breakfast and with the sound of the slamming backdoor, we would turn our reinvigorated energies into a myriad of outdoor adventures.

A stick that had been shed by the recent winds would suddenly become Excalibur, the legendary sword of King Arthur, emblazoned with the benefits of its magical powers, with which Jerry and I would destroy legions of barbarians; or that stick became the only device with which I could save the life of my friend who had become hopelessly mired in a pool of quicksand.

The sun, the rain and the wind were our constant natural companions, I can still recall the wonderful smell of burning leaves in the fall and the countless hours spent piling up those discarded vestiges of summer and jumping headlong into that pile of beautiful dry color.

Hot summer days were spent at LaFollette Park, swimming in the pool and then swinging ourselves so high that when you had obtained the highest point of your arc, at that precise moment when gravity was about to pull you back towards the ground, you experienced an awesome sensation of being weightless. Yes, those were glorious days to be a child and to have blessed friends with which to share those days, those moments, those memories.

So, after an imaginative day of play at my house, Jerry asked my mother if I could spend the night at his house. After inhaling our food. We left the house filled with high spirits and a renewed sense of electric anticipation.

The sun had not yet put itself to bed and the walk to Jerry's house was pleasant and exciting. We arrived at my friend's house and after the usual question and answer conversation with his parents about my well-being and the general health of the rest of my family, we got down to some serious play. I loved going over to Jerry's house, his mother was always kind and loved pushing food at us, which I relished as much as a fat man, holding tray at his favorite buffet. His father would be in the living room reading the newspaper and I sure didn't mind gawking at his lovely older sister.

Here is where the stupidity theory starts to get revved up. We went down into the depths of his darkened basement and after scrounging around for toys, he came across a pair of dart guns. We quickly found some hiding places and began to hunt each other down, firing rubber tipped darts whenever a fraction of our bodies became exposed. After about thirty minutes of play, Jerry and I decided it would be a lot more fun and daring if we removed the rubber tips. And if removing the rubber tips was not daring enough, we also decided to sharpen the dull round plastic tip into a sharp spiral by rubbing the tips on the concrete floor.

The actual ability to draw blood raised the level of play to something akin to being cast into an action packed 007 movie. I remember I was hiding behind the furnace and I had just caught Jerry performing a well-executed low crawl to a more desirable location. While trying to keep one eye on his progress and at the same time trying to load the dart into the pistol is where the pinnacle of the brainlessness theory came into play.

I had pushed the dart down into the yawning, black hole of the pistol using my right hand and just before I removed it, I looked down to make sure I had loaded the pistol correctly.

While staring downward, I removed my hand and the dart shot out the gun and before I could even blink and struck me point first into the center of my right eye. I saw stars and immediately dropped the pistol and I began to vigorously rub my injured eye. I can't remember if I cried out in surprise and pain, but as quick as a parched beer lover downs his first brew of the day, Jerry was standing by my side asking if I was okay.

At first the pain was more of a throbbing and I told Jerry that I was going to be okay. But as the initial shock and numbness to the eye began to wear away, I started to experience a sharp and excruciating pain from my injured body part.

Without a hint, I suddenly turned on the screaming and crying. It would have rivaled the intensity of a fire truck, sirens wailing, as it passed by. I sprinted out of his house and made a beeline for my home as if the boogey man himself was hot on my heels, all the while holding my right hand over my injured eye.

As I ran and wailed, I could hear the echoes of my screams reverberating blocks away and as I passed houses, lights were suddenly turned on and faces seen, pressed tight against the windows. scanning the darkened night looking for the cause of such a ruckus. Even though I knew my young life was not in mortal danger, I had visions of wearing a black patch over the hollowed-out eye socket for the rest of my life and any future career choices would be dramatically whittled down to being the pirate host at the local seafood restaurant.

As I bounded up the stairs to our side door, I turned up the volume a few more decibels; this would provide my parents a few more precious seconds of preparation and also increased the chances of garnering more than usual, compassion and mercy.

It took my mother about five minutes of chasing me down once I entered the house, it seems my legs and feet were in no hurry to stop, I guess they were still in survival mode and seeing I had made a few trips to the emergency room already, my legs were not going to stop until the smell of bleach and iodine indicated their arrival to such a facility.

I then remember being in Doctor's Cherkasky's office and he was examining my eye with a bright light and a pair of magnifying glasses perched upon his nose, all the while chastising me for not being more careful. And if the dart had penetrated just a few more millimeters, I would have been guaranteed to have lost the sight in my eye.

He then placed some pain killer drops in my injured eye and immediately the pain began to drop in intensity. I had to wear a patch upon that eye for a few weeks and was placed on house arrest until I healed. Did you observe the two basic parts of the stupidity theory in this story? The lower-than-normal IQ quotient and the inability to think beyond one thought at a time. If I had taken the time or the ability to think through the suggestion of removing the rubber tips, I would have recognized the danger of such an action. And If I had, like a good chess player, processed at least two thoughts before removing my hand from the barrel of the dart gun, I would have realized the importance of moving my head out of the way. So, if you ever find yourself over at Jerry's house and he suggests playing a game that involves dart guns; please, wear a good pair of protective eye glasses.

Jerry remained one of my best friends through the years. We graduated from cowboys and Indians, to football, basketball, and track and we shared our adventurous experiences in growing up. He became a well-respected business man in our local community. He was always competitive but yet kind, thoughtful and always encouraging. Whether he spent five minutes or five hours with you, he was always genuinely interested in what you had to say and happy to have spent the time with you. And even though our latter lives were separated by thousands of miles and mired in the hours spent in growing a business and a family, he was always just a phone call or a heartfelt thought away.

● ● ● ●● ● ● ●

I lived on the corner of 7Th and Kenneth Street until I was ten years old. And trust me I had plenty of adventures with my friends and siblings. Some adventures involved Barbie doll breast reductions, rubbing them vigorously on the concrete sidewalks until they were reduced to small piles of shredded plastic, my older sister Gail stills complains that because of me she had the only breast free Barbie's in town. There was another incident involving the girl from across the alley, Louie and me playing army, a huge razor-sharp knife, an interrogation, and a last-minute saving tackle by Louie's father. Even today Louie Verhagen's mother shutters at the thought of what could have happened. As for me, I believe no harm would have befallen the girl, I just wanted to scare her into providing us with some vital military intelligence, so that General Patton could launch his next strategic move.

My residence at this location provided me with the basic building blocks from which future adventures would be built upon. I remember the day as if it happened just yesterday. It was January 28th my tenth birthday. The weather was cold enough to give a penguin a bad case of frost bite. My parents and their friends were busy boxing up possessions and loading pickup trucks. I can recall how bummed out I felt on this birthday because here it was the one day that was supposed to be your special day and yet, nobody seemed to be giving me any special consideration. I just sat down on the one remaining chair left in the kitchen and put on my best pouting face.

Shortly thereafter, mom came by and knelt down beside me and explained that they had not forgotten my birthday and when we got to our new house there would be a birthday cake and some presents awaiting my attention. This new bit of information was what I needed to pick up my sagging spirits and soon I was offering my assistance in packing up the house.

After the last of the household items were loaded into the trucks, we climbed into my father's car and prepared to travel to our new homestead. As we pulled away from the curb, I stared out the rear window of the car watching the only home I had ever known quickly fade away into the distance.

The tears began, at first slowly, and then in increased in volume as I came to realize that my best friend, Louie, was not going to be knocking on my door tomorrow to ask if I could come out to play. Nor would we be communicating about the day's events or tomorrows play from my bedroom window to his bedroom window.

No more summer days spent together at the La Follete park where we swam in the parks pool and turned each other dizzy on the well-worn merry go round. No more sleepovers watching cheesy black and white horror flicks while eating popcorn or Mrs. Verhagen's delicious home-made bread. Everything that I had come to love was fading away as my father's car sped off into the gathering darkness of the winter sunset.

Wiping the streaming tears onto the sleeves of my jacket I turned around and asked the only important question a ten year could utter at that special emotional moment, "are we there yet".

• • ⋯ •• •• • • •

The house my father had just purchased was located on 18th street, a rather new neighborhood, with a drive-in restaurant just three houses away, how can they say God doesn't answer prayers. With that ready and nearby source of mouthwatering, fat saturated, menu of fast-food cuisine, of course the makers of acne products were already beginning to anticipate a banner year. But there were new friends to meet and new adventures to embark upon and best of all, it was only three short city blocks from the country fields and woods that I would come to know and love.

The first year on 18th street passed pretty much like a blur. A new school and new friends had kept me pretty busy. And now the excitement of Christmas and the anticipated holiday vacation was pushing our anticipation rates into high gear. This winter season was throwing out plenty of snow and cold, which provided all of the necessary ingredients for a season of great sledding, ice skating and tobogganing, which also included the possibility of multiple contusions, various cuts and concussions. This plethora of medical attention was greatly anticipated by the town's medical staff, not unlike the highly prized dollars generated in tourist towns during the summer vacation season.

The weekend before, the sleepy little town of Kaukauna, had won the snowfall lottery. A deep glistening layer of snow blanketed the community, which inspired its children to shout with glee and to dream of anticipated sledding exploits, while our fathers drudged through waist deep snow, battling four-foot drifts with large rectangular shovels and muttering something about possible heart attacks and insurance policies.

I awoke the following Friday morning at the same time an ice storm was blowing through town. The crystallized water left a sheet of ice on everything it touched. Seeing our parents had already left for work and at the rate most city employees cleared and salted the roads, I had about six hours of unsupervised fun. Looking out the living room at the newly formed ice-skating rink, I observed that my friend, Tommy, was also looking out his living room window with the same expression that most burglars, when scanning a room full of priceless antiques, have frozen upon their faces.

After frantically waving my hands for a few minutes, Tommy finally saw my gestures of attention and motioned me to come on over to his house. Throwing on my winter coat, gloves, hat and boots, I gingerly walked, fell and slid myself over to Tommy's house. After raiding his parent's refrigerator for any tantalizing leftovers, we excitedly discussed what our first excursion into the freshly made over winter wonderland should be. We decided on taking advantage of an opportunity that comes once in a blue moon, a rare priceless meteorological event that allows children to ice skate miles of ice coated city streets, instead of being confined to the few local ice-skating rinks situated throughout the town.

Donning our ice skates, we proceeded to glide effortlessly down the empty, ice encased, city streets, marveling at the beautiful landscape created by Mother Nature's wintry hand. After cruising what seemed like miles of icy roads, we turned our red cheeked faces into the cold wind and skated for home.

After drinking a couple of mugs of hot chocolate that turned my mother's kitchen into a filthy, sticky, chocolate covered mess, we began recounting the rare memories we had just formed when suddenly an idea struck my brain with the force of a locomotive striking a ford pinto broadside. I have often wondered about the source of such ideas; the usual course of such sudden and powerful cranial events ended up in severe and lengthy punishments bestowed upon me by my mother or father. Maybe, the houses my dad bought was built upon ancient Indian burial grounds where I could be, at times, victimized by the ghosts of long dead and pissed off warriors. Or maybe, I was being manipulated, unawares, by the evil forces and temptations of Satan and his evil dominions. Nah, the probable answer lies in the depths and complexity of human nature and fetal development. Probably, at the time when mom was baking me in the oven of her womb, God asked me about brains and I thought he said trains and I said "I'll take me a slow one".

There is a rule among young boys, that when you are about to do something stupid and dangerous, make sure it has creativity and glamour enough as to warrant childhood sainthood, just in case the end result either leaves you vacant eyed and drooling for the rest of your life or you find yourself becoming fertilizer in the towns cemetery.

It's also amazing how ideas quickly take on a life of their own. The intricate details of the adventure flowed out as natural as maple syrup in the spring. After a brief recess to further decimate the food remains of my mother's kitchen, Tommy and I sprang into action.

The plan was simple but yet exciting. To the best of our knowledge, no one in our neighborhood had yet attempted such a feat. Thus, it fulfilled the unique component of a daring adventure. We were going to attempt to ride a toboggan down a flight of indoor stairs, through the open front door, across the front porch, shoot over the front sidewalk, landing upon the ice encrusted four feet of snow in the front yard, shoot across the shoveled sidewalk, land onto the ice encased four feet of snow covered terrace, fly onto the ice covered road, with enough speed and momentum to carry us up Tommy's ice encrusted driveway and hopefully come to a screeching stop inside Tommy's garage. Not as extravagant or as well planned as an Evil Knevel motorcycle jump, but impressive enough for the local band of neighborhood kids.

After bracing the front door open and hauling the two-man toboggan up the stairway that led to my sister Gail's and my bedroom, we positioned the toboggan on the landing and seated ourselves upon the gleaming wood slats of the toboggan. Staring down the carpeted covered stairs, we focused all of our attention at the bright spot that marked the opening of the front door. Any deviation left or right would result in a crash that could have dire physical consequences along with devastating damage to the interior wall of the house, which would leave me unable to sit for at least a week after dad got through with me.

The probability of a successful run was marred by a plethora of miscalculations or misfortunes. If we did not build up enough speed down the interior flight of steps, we would not carry over the shoveled front walk and end up in a wood splintering crash into the hard as rock pile of ice-covered snow. If we made that first obstacle, the hard steering toboggan may turn sideways as it built up more speed across the slick, snow covered front yard. That could potentially slam us broadside into the icy pile of snow of the terrace.

If you have ever seen an out-of-control toboggan careen off course and plow into a tree, you can begin to understand the dire consequences we faced if we did not control the trajectory of our toboggan across the front yard. If we managed to successfully navigate that obstacle, the third would be rapidly staring us down. If the path of the sled was either pitched too high or too low, the resulting crash onto the roadway would have the same result as Jeff Gordon slamming his number 20 race car into the wall at high speed.

The last obstacle was our ability to stop the toboggan once we reached the inside of Tommy's garage. If we had built up too much speed, the friction coefficient of the concrete garage floor might not be sufficient enough to bring us to a stop and we would crash hard into the back wall of his garage. With the sound of our hearts beating wildly in our ears; we teetered the toboggan over the landing and plunged down the stairs.

We were pleased with the amount of speed we gathered as we slid down the stairway while the light of the opened front door was rapidly approaching. In a flash we hit the front stoop and like the graceful flight of a ski jumper we flew airborne over the front walk and landed rather lightly onto the snow-covered front yard. Without falter, the toboggan gathered even more speed across the icy glaze of the front yard and shot across the crevasse of the sidewalk with ease. We hit the snow-covered terrace and in a split second we were again airborne heading for a landing upon the ice-covered street. The exhilaration of being briefly airborne and defying the physical bounds of gravity is a feeling that is very difficult to describe, but it is a feeling that always brings you back for more. Kind of like the adrenaline rush a parachutist must feel when rushing towards the earth and then landing safely minutes later.

We did hit the road at the proper angle where the toboggan shuttered just briefly and quickly began to pick up even more speed. We shot up Tommy's driveway and headed for the opened garage door. The moment we reached the dry concrete floor of the garage; the toboggan began to screech and vibrate as it started to shed its speed and momentum.

The front of the toboggan was slowing faster than the rear of the toboggan causing the tail of the toboggan to begin to slide away from the center line of our travel path. The back wall of the garage was drawing nearer as the toboggan sought to shed its remaining momentum and with a final shudder the toboggan halted mere inches away from the garage wall.

We had done it, just like a bobsled team that had just finished a medal winning run, we jumped off the sled and began to high five and danced around the garage, relishing that fleeting moment of glory from a win so justly deserved.

Unfortunately, kids have a bad sense of timing. We continued that toboggan run a little too long. Maybe it was the icicles hanging from the living room lamps or the frozen glass of milk on the kitchen table that was the giveaway. Leaving the front door open for hours that cold winter day was definitely not an Einstein moment for me.

The painful lecture from my father was not enough to diminish our accomplishment that day nor the accolades bestowed upon us by our peers, besides, my dad promised me that my grounding would expire by the time the dog woods blossomed come spring.

．．．．．． ．．．．． ．．． ．

As a young child, I quickly came to recognize and choose which fruits and vegetables I would love to eat and which varieties would make me gag at the mere sight of them. Not to mention the feud my mother and I had for years over the consumption of cooked carrots.

I would be sitting at the kitchen table, usually hours after everyone else had eaten, staring at that cooling pile of orange vegetable matter, while my mother demanded that before I could leave, I had to consume all of those mushy, orange, disgusting carrots.

In my mind's eye, it must have been the same disgusting sensation Socrates felt while staring at the hemlock poison that he was required to drink as punishment for his political activities. But of all of the fruits and vegetables that I came to love, watermelon was to become the one that I loved the most.

My grandmother worked at the local Piggly Wiggly store as the produce manager and she would keep me informed on the scheduled arrival of those large, red tinted, juice dripping, seed spitting delicacies. Days before the wooden crated melons would arrive, my salivary glands would begin to constantly excrete, causing my mother great concern and inciting threats about another dose of Castor oil.

But every year at that terrestrial moment in time I would begin to sharpen my ability to discern the ripeness of a watermelon by rapping inanimate objects and then keenly listen to the reverberating sound waves it produced, not unlike a highly trained naval sonarman, listening intently for any unnatural sounds that would disclose the presence of an enemy vessel. The next training step was to wait until my mother went to the store so I could practice on lesser fruit such as cantaloupe and honeydew melons.

Early on, I unfortunately discovered that tomatoes were a poor source for practice. The delicate fruit, wait a minute, I mean vegetable, hold on now, are they a fruit or a vegetable. The scientific community could settle the matter by qualifying them as a vegefruit. This would certainly help in dispersing the many arguments concerning this passion fruit, I mean vegetable, damn I meant fruit. Anyway, the first time I placed a good thumping on this tomato, the skin caved in immediately and the thick, sticky, pulp sprayed out in all directions, which of course, some of that sticky goo came to rest upon myself and the unfortunate lady standing adjacent to me.

[47]

It seems that tomato pulp, although enjoyed on and in all types of foods and salads, does not have the same enjoyment when wearing it upon your clothes. After the menacing threats issued from my mom mostly of "don't make me take you outside, because outside there are no witnesses", I was made to apologize to the newly fruited lady and then given a very short leash for the rest of the shopping spree. So, to all of you young inspiring melon thumpers, be warned, stay away from tomatoes.

All that practice was funneled into one important task, to search for and identify the most delicious, juicy and sweet melons out of the bunch. As a matter of fact, I was considered by my family and friends as the official expert watermelon thumper.

Many a day, I was called away from my usual senseless activity to confirm someone's watermelon choice. Now, this passion for watermelon led me to a series of unfortunate events which would haunt me for years to come, not to mention the cold, sweat induced, nightmares I would experience on those summer nights that coincided with the harvest of that addicting fruit. Unfortunately, Doctor Phil was still in the process of going through puberty and was not yet available for the deep and honest professional help he is so associated with today.

Anyway, back to the story. It was a most unusual day, we had just come back from the community pool, where we had enjoyed harassing the life guards and parading around for the lovely, young ladies. I had just finished eating my supper, thank the good lord no cooked carrots that night, and I was sitting quietly on the front porch. This was our secret signal to any of the neighborhood friends that I was now available for any possible evening shenanigans.

It wasn't long before I heard a front door slam and the sound of rubber soled sneakers pounding across the hot asphalt street. Looking up, I saw Norman running towards me with that exaggerated smile on his face which could only mean one thing, trouble.

After leaping up the two concrete steps of our front porch, he quickly settled into a sitting position where he promptly began to spill his conspiracy. I listened intently for some time and then I began to inquire about his previous whereabouts and why he had not gone to the pool with the rest of us. He started to babble on about spending the day in the nearby woods and that he had come across a great discovery. With renewed attention, I eagerly awaited the description of the newly found discovery and even expressed my committed attention with a few nods of my head and few well timed huh, huhs. He explained that after a few hours of catching crayfish he had decided to get up and do a little exploring.

Following an unused and dilapidated barbed wire fence, he walked into an unfamiliar area of the woods and had discovered an old house, probably built around the time George Washington was wintering at Valley Forge. At that point, I began to drift away from his conversation, discovering an old house situated in the middle of the woods was not earth-shattering news nor was it, in my mind, the subject of a great discovery. But out of the flow of his insistent babble a single word reached the hairlike fibers of my inner ear while traveling at the speed of sound, it quickly reached the interpreter portion of my brain. That word was, you guessed it, watermelon. The occupant of that old house had a garden and a large portion of that garden was dedicated to growing large, sweet, juicy watermelons.

The next morning Norman and I went to pay the new discovery a visit. Using our best military maneuvers, a two-man reconnaissance strategy, we approached the garden undetected. I could not believe my eyes, there spread out before me was a treasure trove of home-grown watermelons. The desire to push aside all concerns of safety and run wild eyed into that vast garden of watermelon beauties was almost more than I could bear. My thumping finger began to twitch uncontrollably, not unlike the trigger finger of a western gunman just before he drew his pistol at a high noon showdown.

Now low crawling, we positioned ourselves into the middle of the garden and then drawing myself up into a kneeling position, I excitedly began thumping watermelons and after about a dozen attempts, I heard the most beautiful sound reverberate back into my ears, a perfectly ripe watermelon. Excitedly, I pulled out my pocketknife and began to cut through the tough, sinewy stem that separated that prize watermelon from yours truly

As I was just finishing separating the vine from that glorious watermelon, I suddenly heard Norman shout, "Bob looks out". Looking up at Norman, I turned my face in the direction where his now wide and bulging eyes were locked onto and staring intently.

There standing about twenty feet away was a rather plumb, gray haired elderly women whose face was now twisted into a mask of rage and the words that flowed out of her mouth was not exactly a conversation you would over hear at a Sunday worship service. In a mixture of English and German, spoken with a strong German accent, she was loudly sputtering, "Hey you kleine sheisseren, legen das watermelon, bereits Ich blow your kopf off und get sie arsch out of meine garten". Now growing up with a grandmother who spoke fluent German I could piece together the message she was trying to convey, as I had heard some of those words spoken to me quite often. But unfortunately, Norman being of Dutch Ancestry did not have a clue as to what she was saying.

But the expression on her face and the tone in which she was speaking left no doubt that she wanted us out of her watermelon patch. Grabbing the watermelon and carrying it under my arm like a football, I sprang up and as I was turning to run, I saw the plump elderly women raise an object and place it against her shoulder. In an instant, I recognized that object and it filled me with terror; I was suddenly looking down the barrels of a well-oiled, side by side twelve-gauge shotgun, which to say the least increased the velocity of my hasty retreat by at least mach ten.

After sprinting across the green, broad leafed watermelon garden, I placed my focus on the barbed wire fence and a particular post on that barbed wire fence. Upon reaching that post and without breaking stride, I placed my left hand on the top of the post and using the post as leverage, vaulted myself over the sagging top wire.

As I was sailing over the top of the loose barbed wire, a loud explosion filled the air and my body was suddenly pelted with what felt like a thousand angry bee stings. The impact sent me reeling head first into the soft, leaf littered, soil of the woods and after a few deaccelerating somersaults I came to a painful stop. Lying on my back, I became acutely aware of my ragged labored breathing, my racing heart rate and the intense sound of blood rushing through my ears. I could not believe what my brain was screaming out, that that seemly harmless little old lady had just pumped me full of buckshot.

Now the normal dress of the day, for most boys, were faded jeans with the cuffs rolled up and a plain white t-shirt. Looking down, I noticed that my bleached, white t-shirt was now covered in last year's foliage and large spots of red that were slowly spreading across the cotton material. Jumping up I ran towards Norman screaming that I had been shot and that the possibility of me living to see the next tick of the hour hand on my wrist watch was rapidly becoming extremely poor.

Both Norman and I ran through the woods weeping and screeching that we had been shot and that we were in the process of dying. We ran until we reached the bend in the creek where we normally spent our time fishing for crawdads or skinny dipping. There we stopped and quickly stripped off our clothes. Expecting to see huge ugly holes pouring out the essence of our young lives, we were happily surprised to see instead, huge, red welts developing across our buttocks, legs and lower back.

The red sticky spots that had spread across our t-shirts, that we thought was blood, was actually the juice of the watermelon that had broken open when we had landed clumsily, hard upon them.

With the sudden realization that we were not going to expire, we both lay upon the ground allowing our shaking bodies the ability to return back to a more normal state. Looking up at the beautiful blue sky I was overcome with the joy that comes with the anticipation of a life yet to live and was grateful that instead of buckshot, that elderly women had blasted us with two shotgun rounds loaded with rock salt.

You may think that was an unusual and mean method of deterring young boys from stealing her watermelons, but I can attest to the fact that Norman nor I ever stole another watermelon from that grey-haired women's garden. I never told my parents of this event, because in those days on top of the painful welts from the rock salt, I would have received a spanking for trespassing and attempting to steal someone's private property. Besides, after a month of sitting awkwardly and walking rather stiff, I was to have a complete recovery.

Maybe, especially in today's politically correct parental child rearing environment, a little well-placed rock salt would go a long way in providing some children a valuable lesson in ethics.

• • • •• • • •

When your eleven years old, the most trusted form of transportation is your bicycle. It's faster than walking and it can be upgraded to portray your individualism. Kids would adorn their bikes with colored plastic trailers, that when placed into the end of the handlebars, would coolly flutter in the breeze as you pedaled down the street. Packets of baseball or football cards were inserted between the spokes of the bicycles tires and held in place with clothes pins. The humming sound of those cards was as revered as the unique sound of a Harley Davidson as it growled down the road. One of the benefits of a bike was its ability to decrease the arrival time to reach your destination like the Kaukauna public pool. The usual thirty-minute walk was cut down to around fifteen minutes. Most of us cared for our bikes just like most adults cared for their car. Periodic cleanings and maintenance would guarantee you a reliable ride, but it also invoked the competitive spirit found lurking in the souls of young boys.

Racing each other home was a form of establishing the athletic pecking order. I usually finished a respectable second or third place in most races but I also had my occasional brush with the painful condition called road rash. Once, while flying down one of the steepest hills in town, where the Kaukauna Club Cheese factory used to be located, I attempted to apply the brake on my bike. In those days the brake was located only on the rear wheel and you had to push the pedals hard backwards to engage them. The strap that held the Bendix brake arm to the lower frame of the bike suddenly broke loose and at that moment, I no longer had a mechanical means by which to stop my bike.

Approaching the first major intersection of town, at break neck speed, I had to apply the only form of alternate braking methodology, my tennis shoes. Quickly jumping off my seat, I straddled the top bike frame and pushed the bottom of my tennis shoes hard against the pavement. The high-pitched scream of an adolescent boy, coupled with the smell of burning red ball jets was now permeating the hot summer breeze. With just inches to spare, I came to a stop at the busy intersection and barely missed becoming a bloody and mangled form of myself by a 64 Chevy pickup.

After a morning of fruitful play, we all decided to thwart the rising summer heat by spending the afternoon in the cold waters of the city pool, chasing young girls, splashing lifeguards and cannon balls off of the high dive.

After we met at Dick's Drive Inn; we started our joyous journey to the public pool. Usually, the first person in the pack would decide which bike route was going to be used to reach our final destination. On this day, the point man was taking us to the access road located at the end of Seventh Street.

Once we made the right turn onto Seventh Street, you could feel the race excitement begin to build. Our pace speed started to pick up and the boys were beginning to jockey for positions in the pack. I was in fourth position and was trying to get around Randy, but he kept blocking my attempts. I faked a pass to his right and when he changed his course to block me, I quickly turned and passed him on his left, a maneuver that most NASCAR drivers use today. I was now behind the leaders, Kenny in first position with his younger brother Normy in second position. As we approached the end of Seventh Street, we could see the shiny chrome traffic barrier quickly approaching. This was the best opportunity to better my pole position. There was small opening on the left side just big enough for a single bicycle to pass through. Just as Normy slowed down to squeeze through the small opening, I performed a pit maneuver on him and positioned myself right behind the leader. Once through the opening, I began to pedal as fast as I could, resulting in maximizing my descent speed. Halfway down the steep course I was still neck n neck with Kenny. As we flashed past the three-quarter mark, I pulled a bicycle length ahead of Kenny. In all of the bike races we competed in, I had never won a race going down that access road, until this summer day. I could not believe it; I was actually going to win this prestigious racing event.

As we approached the bottom of the hill a quick decision had to be made; you could go straight and cross the three sets of railroad tracks or you could push hard on the brake and perform a sliding left turn. I tried desperately to stop but the pedals were turning to fast. When we reached the bottom of the hill, Kenny turned hard left onto the access road, but I kept moving straight ahead. After I had shed enough speed, I placed my feet upon the spinning pedals and regained control. With a victor's grin spreading from ear to ear, I thrust my arms straight up into the sky to publicly broadcast my hard-won victory.

But on this day fate had a cruel twist in store. As I sped through the tall grass, I suddenly spotted three iron rails laying across the single dirt path, and before I could react, my front tire struck the first steel rail with an incredible force. The sudden deceleration of the front end of my bike sent the back of my bike into an aggressive forward somersault. I was sent cascading through the air as if I had been shot out of a circus cannon. Looking back, there have been a few times in my life, where I believe with all my heart, that a guardian angel had intervened and had prevented a dreadful injury or death itself and this was one of those times.

As I rocketed towards the ground, I could see that my potential landing zone was the second set of rail road tracks. Without the benefit of any safety gear, I surmised that once my head impacted one of those steel rails, that I would be instantly trading in my bike for a set of wings and a harp. But as the steel rails rushed towards me and death waited, I felt my body become completely rigid and it turned approximately ninety degrees as if guided by a pair of invisible hands. I landed squarely between the rails and slid to a stop with my back, now bruised and bleeding, up against the far rail.

Now even though God had spared me from a lifetime of crayons and coloring books or worse yet an everlasting dirt nap, he did not spare me from an important and painful life lesson. I remember lying between those rails with the blood of a plethora of cuts running down my face and arms; the right side of my body painful and tingling, I could hear the screams of the crossing guard who had witnessed my accident.

I remember my friends running over and asking me if I was alright and then proceeded to help me to my feet. As I walked over to the crossing guard, she asked if we needed to call an ambulance. I mumbled that I would be okay and continued on to the pool. I soaked my wounds in the cold water, as I watched my friends chase the young girls, engage in chicken fights and cannon ball life guards, as they sat perched upon their rescue towers.

For the rest of my childhood, every time my friends raced down that access road, I slowly and safely brought up the rear. Dancing with the grim reaper that day had completely extinguished any desire to reach for the bike racing brass ring. It was not the end of my youthful competitiveness; I would just have to focus that energy into other arenas of competition.

• • ••• • •• • • • •• • •

It's amazing how at certain age levels, boys instinctively develop specific propensities towards specific behaviors. For example; boys between the ages of two and three suddenly come to the realization that they have a special appendage and for the next few years, they spend hours every day with their hands down their pants making sure the damn thing had not fallen off. My three boys, when they had reached that peculiar age, were constantly being reassured by their mother, especially in public places, that the special appendage was still attached and could they please stop fondling it in public. Next, come's the cowboy and Indian phase, where after spending a few hours watching their favorite western TV hero reduce the criminal population to a more manageable level, boys would descend upon their neighborhoods with all the energy of a cat strung out on catnip, chasing, ambushing and quick drawing everything and everybody in sight.

After that phase, comes the pre-athletics phase. This is where the brain and the body of a young boy are attempting to develop some form of coordination. The instinctual behaviors, at this stage, are beginning to become quite apparent. Incidents of broken windows and busted street lamps are suddenly on the rise. A stone on the roadway or sidewalk now takes on a new and exciting value, the value of a projectile.

A boy in this phase will pick up that stone, roll it around in the palm of his hand, and then, scanning the nearby horizon, pick out a target, usually a tree, a street sign or a street lamp. The damaged windows are usually the result of a novice who is still attempting to developing their ability to drive tacks into a tree at thirty paces or to chip the paint out of the letter O on a stop sign. In this phase, boys spend hours developing their ability to accurately hit targets with whatever fits inside their small hands, stones, mud balls, snow balls, marbles, and even rotten vegetables.

Hey, remember boys at this age are too young to work so they have to usually forage for their projectiles of opportunity. It was not uncommon, that at construction sites, boys would pair off into teams and with ammunition supplies at a premium, would actively engage in mud ball combat. Picking off your enemy with a well-aimed mud ball was a prized ability and usually saved you from a couple of large welts obtained by the opposing team. It was in this phase where this adventure takes place and it involves a vegetable once called the love apple, the amazing tomato.

It had been an unusual rainy summer; the creeks were running at capacity and the local gardens were swimming in rainfall. The neighbor behind our house was quite a gardener. He had most of his backyard and the empty lot next to him tilled up in perfect furrows which were planted with a plethora of vegetable varieties. Unfortunately, his tomato crop, from all of the rain, had turned too soft and mushy. The pile of those discarded vegetable projectiles now laid upon the edge of his garden and the temptation was too much to bear for those of us deep within the pre-athletic phase.

Once my friends and I had spotted that massive pile of rotting food matter, the seeds of mischief were quickly planted, fertilized and harvested. Our plan was, once it became dark, we would sneak over to our neighbor's house and fill our paper grocery bags with as much ammunition that those bags could hold. Once we were fully supplied, a debate ensued over the best use of such an uncommon and blessed opportunity. We settled on this particular battle plan. We would flank both sides of 18th street, hiding between the houses, with a point man concealed in the front bushes providing advanced warning of any approaching targets.

As I remember, it was a beautiful night, the full moon combined with the luminescence of the soft street lamps provided a Hollywood movie atmosphere to the quiet landscape. My assigned position was to the east side of my house where I was supported by another member of our team, Tommy Reinholtz. I could not have had a better support person covering my six, he was gifted, he could take a fly off a post from thirty feet.

The first unsuspecting car that passed our ambush location was quickly turned from a clean and gleaming automobile to a colorful and slimy advertisement for tomato paste. The drivers would become confused and dazed at first but after a few moments the reality of the situation would sink in and they would become quite angry. The sound of screeching tires would be our cue to beat feet and put some distance between ourselves and the victim of that tomato pasting thus making proper criminal identification rather difficult. As we fled, the rapid and loud barrage of curses would only make our guffaws and laughter that much more deeply shared and satisfying.

After successfully ambushing three unsuspecting citizens, we took a well-deserved break and headed down to Dick's Drive In for some celebratory ice cream. You may be unaware but throwing dozens of juicy, rotting, tomatoes at moving automobiles is sweat inducing work and the raucous laughter that ensues tends to parch one's throat. After the usual rehashing of our successful exploit's, we headed back to our predetermined ambush positions for one last mission of the evening.

Soon, the high-pitched sound of a three fifty Honda dirt bike became progressively louder, and as the unsuspecting motorcycle enthusiast rushed closer into our area, we prepared ourselves. It was imperative that you know exactly when to expose your position and to allow for the correct amount of lead on a moving target.

As soon as that motorcycle reached our ambush position, we began to pelt that poor slob with a mass of slimy, red vegetable matter, until he represented the poster child for a Hunt's ketchup commercial. At the highest point of our exhilaration, we witnessed a most spectacular event. Instead of the usual slowing down and the uttering of colorful cuss words, this victim, with the grace of a seasoned motorcycle racer, slide the bike to a controlled stop in the middle of the street and met our gazes with a look of revenge that turned one's blood ice cold.

Fixing his hateful gaze upon us, he revved his motorcycle and then, at full throttle, launched his mechanical steed at us. It's amazing that when the hunter suddenly becomes the hunted how time seems too dramatically slow down. It was like watching an African wildlife documentary where the lion is chasing the impala in slow motion. Or those nightmares as a young child, when walking through a fogged filled forest and suddenly the frightful beast of your imagination springs out into the night filled darkness. You attempt to run but your legs are mired in quicksand and the beast gains ground with every toothy stride. And now I was the gazelle and the rider was the lion.

Anyway, as Tom and I sprinted away from the approaching motorcycle madman, who was clearly intent upon transforming our bodily forms into deep bloody and earthly impressions. In that moment, the tingling feeling of fear surged strongly through our veins and then in an instant, completely engulfed us. As I looked over my shoulder, I noticed, grimly, that the motorcycle was rapidly gaining ground, and as we ran through backyards and through gardens, the rider continued to bore revengefully down upon us, disregarding any private property. It seemed his only attention was focused on inflicting as much damage to our young bodies as he possibly could muster.

I could hear the high-pitched whine of the engine as the front tire of the motorcycle was now within inches of my back side. I could imagine the intense, maniacal look upon his face, his eyes narrowed and unblinking, his face twisted into a mask of contorted rage, his moment of revenge now just mere inches away.

At the last second, I hollered to Tommy to break right, it was one of our favorite moves, if our pursuer was tight on our heels one of us would break hard right while the other would break hard left. It always provided a perfect moment for escape. The pursuer had to suddenly make a decision on whom he wanted to continue chasing, this pause allowed us to gain momentum and distance. And as soon as I had spoken the command, Tommy made a hard left turn while I broke right.

The motorcycle attempted to adjust to the sudden maneuver but began to decelerate quickly which caused him to momentarily lose control of his motor bike. Which allowed me to speed away running straight for the wooden fence that separated the two back yards.

With the agility of a gymnast, I hit the ground hard and immediately rolled under the bottom board of the fence. My momentum carried me to a position under a large cedar tree but now with the manmade barrier positioned between my pursuer and myself, I was safe for the moment.

Crawling out from under the large canopy of the soft needled cedar; I was suddenly confronted by the property owner, an elderly gentleman. In a tone and language typical of the day, he spoke, "What the hell are you doing under my cedar tree, you little bast—d". And in the typical fashion of the time period, I gave him my response, a toothy grin and a brief glimpse of my backside as I ran between his house and his neighbors.

After hiding in my dad's brother's back yard for around an hour, I slowly made my way back to the original scene of the ambush, half expecting the crazed rider to suddenly appear from out of the shadows. Upon reaching Tommie's house I gave the all-clear whistle which we used as a signal so that the rest of the gang could leave their hiding places and rendezvous at our designated spot.

At the gathering, Tommy and I excitedly retold our harrowing tale and the narrow escape from the motorcycle rider from hell. It was at the end of our story that I heard my mother's voice ring out calling for my return, a bath and then bedtime. With a sigh of disappointment, I said my good nights to my friends and then headed for home.

After a hot bath and a good washing behind my ears, I settled myself down between the clean and cool sheets of my bed. As I lay there staring up at the ceiling, I pondered the events of the night. I could not help but feel a slight pain of guilt for what had transpired. I even began to understand the behavior of our two wheeled victim. And even though he had fallen short of his intended punishment, the lesson he taught us that night did not go unheeded nor forgotten.

From that day on, cars, trucks and even municipal vehicles were considered fair game, but we never again attempted to ambush riders on a motorcycle.

• • • •• • •• • • • • •• • • ••• • ••• •

The luminescence from the TV screen flickered randomly around the darkened living room; as though you were watching a passing thunderstorm. It was early Saturday morning and I was watching another spell binding episode of Tom and Jerry. And, as usual, Tom was getting his butt kicked by the smaller rodent name Jerry.

At that time, I was puzzled by the idea that a mouse who was far inferior in physical size and brain mass, could consistently outwit the cat who was far superior in physical size and brain mass. Besides, the natural world dictated that the predator usually had the upper hand in capturing and devouring its prey. Ah the cartoon world, as funny and entertaining as it is, it seems to be totally devoid of representing the realities of the real world.

Seconds later, my television trance was painfully interrupted by the sudden wails of my older sister insisting that I had, maliciously and with evil intent, performed a radical mastectomy on yet another one of her Barbie dolls by attempting to rub those protruding, hard plastic representations off on the concrete sidewalk, my form of karma.

After a few minutes of unsuccessful denials and attempted bribes, I hastily exited the living room before Mom became involved in the squabble. Mom was about thirteen years into parenthood and was in the transition stage from quietly and verbally trying to resolve our issues, to charging into the room while speaking some strange form of pig Latin and threatening to beat us to within an inch of our lives.

By the time the hinges on the screened back door had stopped screeching, I was already around the back corner of our house and was headed towards a friend's house located just across the street. It was early spring in Wisconsin and this Saturday had dawned clear and warm. As a matter of fact, the entire week had been unusually dry and warm, there were only scatterings of snow piles and those were located under considerable shady areas.

The ice on the creek at the end of our street had been broken up by an earlier wind storm which piled up the fragmented remnants onto the banks of the cold, running, creek. It was a perfect day to explore the woods and fields that stretched for miles at the end of our street, allowing us to transform ourselves into the many characters of our play world. Maybe today we would be courageous soldiers storming the beaches at Normandy, or treacherous pirates pillaging the British Crown's merchant vessels or wild animals chasing down our elusive, frightened prey. With our spirits high and our imaginations boundless, my friends and I set off to discover what awaited us in that magical stretch of forest.

After playing a rigorous game of the fox and hounds, we ended up walking slowly along the creek banks sifting through the winter refuse to see if the winter ice had vomited up any treasures of interest. We came to a bend in the creek where the city garbage dump was located when, suddenly, a chipmunk darted out from between one of our friend's feet and as soon as that chipmunk had exposed itself, the chase was on. But the chipmunk proceeded to run and hide inside a large hollowed out log not more than twenty or thirty feet away. Never being more than mere feet behind the little critter during the chase, we knew with absolute certainty that the chipmunk had not emerged from the opposite end of the log.

With some of us guarding each end of the hollow log, to prevent its escape, we began to deliberate a plan on how to capture this furry little critter. After rummaging around the garbage dump, we managed to dig up two pieces of canvass that would work at preventing the chipmunk from attempting to leave his fibrous hideout.

After we had the canvas pieces in place, we discovered a hole in our plan, there was no ingenious idea on how to lure our rodent of interest out of his woody fortress. Taking a time out, we debated the many diabolical choices of rousting out our prey. We finally decided the best plan was to stuff one end of the log with dead sticks, twigs and grass; and then, with the sulfur scent of a wooden match, we would proceed to set the one end of the log on fire. Knowing now that the chipmunk had only one safe exit, we all gathered around the opposite end of the log to await the chipmunk's departure. It was like watching a nature program, imagine, six boys all standing at the end of that log like a pride of lion's, behaviorally posturing, with their muscles all a quiver over the anticipation of enjoying a fresh catch.

As the smoke billowed out of both ends, our anticipation began to waver as the minute hand ticked away on our wrist watches. Thoughts, strange thoughts, started to creep around the fringes of our young developing brains. Thoughts that started to take on communicative properties in the form of speech. I made a statement proclaiming that chipmunks must be able hold their breath for extended periods of time, just like dolphins or whales, utilizing a secret air pocket for occasions such as this. Heads nodded slowly in agreement. Another boy threw out his strange thought by suggesting that the chipmunk may have picked the better of two horrible choices and demonstrated the bushido code of the World War II Japanese soldiers and committed suicide rather than give himself up to the torturous whims of his captors. And before another strange thought could be mustered and uttered, a cry of terror arose from one of the boys in the background.

Turning our heads in the direction of the terrified cry, we gasped in shock and fear. The recently smoldering log had burst into four-foot flames dancing wildly into the warm spring air. Sprinting into action, we all raced for the ice chunks that were littering the banks of the creek. With no bucket or pail to carry any creek water, we picked up chunks of ice and raced back to the burning log. Huge clouds of steam arose every time we dumped the solidified pieces of frozen water on the roaring fire. For a split second it seemed we were getting the upper hand on the fire and its tongues of flames momentarily withered but then would suddenly roar back to life with a renewed vigor as it consumed more and more dry wood. Standing bent over and gasping for breath we came to the horrible realization that we were losing the battle on this brush fire and our next best strategy was to beat a hasty retreat. In mere minutes the surrounding dry grass and brush burst into flames and starting racing up the hillside in its unquenchable desire for more fuel. With the literal fiery demons of hell hot on our heels, we ran like kids pursued by none other than Satan himself.

After reaching the summit of the hill, where we usually took a breather, we continued our frenzy pace until we reached the house of one of our friends whose parents just happened to be out.

After catching our breath, we played a quick game of rock, paper scissors to determine which one of us would be placing the emergency call to the fire department. We may have been a little slow in the uptake but we did have a sprouting sense of responsibility.

The unlucky winner of that game dialed the fire department and in his best imitation of Mr. Ed, the talking horse, described the ferocious nature of the fire and its location.

Within minutes, the ear-piercing screams of the fire trucks started to ring closer and closer as we all piled out the front door to get a close-up glimpse of the fiery red trucks, with their lights flashing, their sirens wailing and the brave firemen dressed in their drab brown fire-resistant suits. We all sat in the backyard of our friend's house keeping tabs on the fire by the amount and height of the black billowing smoke that filled the horizon.

Within an hour, three different fire stations had arrived to combat the blazing fire which consumed about five acres of small trees, dry grass, old rubber tires and winter dried brush. For about a week after the fire, we would prod and sift through the ashes around the burned-out log looking for the boney white skeletal remains of the chipmunk that had eluded us that day.

One day, while brushing away a small pile of ashes from where the bottom of the log had been, I found the evidence that finally answered the puzzling question of the chipmunk's existence. There lying before our feet was a perfect little chipmunk hole, dug out the soft soil beneath this section of the rotting log, an earthen portal to a series of tunnels that ran perhaps a hundred feet in different directions. The blacked stripped rodent had executed his pre-planned route of escape and evasion with military like precision, leaving us higher minded mammals to eventually blacken and char about five acres of woodlot. Not a pretty picture uh.

The very next Saturday morning, I was sitting cross legged on the living room floor, eyes fixated on the screen, watching yet another episode of the Tom and Jerry cartoon. But this time I had a lot more appreciation for Jerry's abilities to outsmart Tom, who was superior in both brain and physical size. If a chipmunk had the ability to outsmart six young boys who were far superior in physical and brain size, then the creators of Tom and Jerry were not totally devoid of representing the realities of life.

And from that time forward, I developed a very healthy respect for matches and the devastation that out-of-control fires create And I would leave the art of fire making to the more capable and responsible adults.

• • • •• • •• • • •• • ••• • •• •••

Have you ever heard the poem, what are little girls are made of, sugar and spice and all's that's nice. Compared to what little boys are made of, frogs and snails and puppy-dog tails. To a ten-year-old boy, little girls are made of cooties, whinnies and afraid to get dirties. My friends and I avoided the girls on our block like they had the plaque. They always wanted us to take time off from our normal duties like, wrestling, playing army, cowboys and Indians, chasing insects or reptiles or just rolling around in the mud, to share in their domestic activities such as, tea parties or playing dolls.

Yikes, the thought of engaging in such activities was akin to being captured by your enemy and without a single threat of torture, spilling your guts about all the sensitive information you possessed. That form of cowardice would have to incur the penalty of death. The only time my older sister could get me to sit down with her and her tea set was when she invoked the wrath of God, which was represented by my mother. And it usually involved at least thirty minutes of my protest mingled with a substantial number of salty tears.

There was only one incident that year that precipitated a miraculous change of attitude toward girls. I was in fourth grade at St. Mary's. It was located about four blocks from my house but the really great attraction was the Hilltop bakery that was located kiddy corner from the school. Every morning Mom would give us ten cents which we would use to buy a doughnut and a carton of milk. This was on top of the wonderful breakfast she would make for us and in those days, without having the luxury of video games, we could easily afford to consume those extra calories because we would burn them off in our daily outdoor play. Life was moving along on the most normal of keels until one fateful Monday morning.

After skipping and chasing each other the four blocks to the bakery, we proceeded to get in line with the rest of the kids, who were waiting anxiously to pick out their glazed beauty. I was scanning the glass enclosed counters deciding on which mouth-watering confection I wanted to sink my teeth into, when I spotted the most beautiful head of golden colored hair. It's glistening, strands of sunshine flowed to below her waist and I found that I could not remove my gaze from upon it. As she turned to converse with an obvious friend standing next to her, I was equally stunned by her beauty.

At that moment, I started to feel physical symptoms for which I had no known previous experience. My heart started to race and my breathing was becoming rapid and shallow. My mouth was becoming dry and I started to tingle in ways I had never tingled before. Now I know the rapid heart rate and dry mouth are common symptoms of many fright or flight experiences, like when the neighbor's dog freed from his steel enclosure would proceed to chase me through my neighborhoods alleys and backyards before I eventually gave him the slip, it was the tingling part of the symptoms that was new and unusual.

As I moved up the line, I could not take my eyes off that golden haired girl. And the closer in proximity the more exaggerated my symptoms became. She was standing in front of the register preparing to pay her bill, when I found myself in an out of body experience, I could hear myself talking and could vaguely feel my body parts moving, it all seemed so far away. The next thing I knew she smiled at me and said a sweet thank you and after she passed by, I looked down to discover my ten cents was no longer in the palm of my hand. I had actually paid for her doughnut and carton of milk. On any normal day it would have taken at least three good size bullies to wrestle away my bakery money but yet here I was, standing, dumbfounded, that I had actually voluntarily given it to a girl, a girl. That was the moment in my young life were my attitude towards girls began to shift.

Her name was Wendy Miller and I had the privilege to get to know her very well. When I was ten, my father purchased a home on 18th street and that golden haired beauty would become one of my closest friends. She lived just two doors from my house and we shared our childhoods, our friends and our dreams. There was many a night when she would knock on my bedroom window and we would just talk for hours about the important issues of our young lives. She even scared the daylights out of me one night when she had crawled through my bedroom window, hid in my closet and proceeded to wait until I was in bed and falling asleep when she started to moan and groan. And when I, with trembling limbs, approached the closet, she leapt out scaring me almost to the point of paralysis.

When she turned seventeen, she heard the most frightening sound of her life, the word cancer. The doctors had discovered she had a very malignant form of skin cancer and her parents were taking her to the Mayo clinic for treatment. I did not see her for quite a while, but when she returned the good news was that they were able to put the cancer into remission. She never shared the painful memories of that stay or the treatments she had received, she was just glad to have her life back.

We finished high school together and she married one of my football teammates and our lives, at that time, would rarely cross paths. The last time I saw Wendy just happened to be an instance of mere luck. A friend of mine wanted me to join him at a summer concert being held near the banks of the Fox River.

After about three hours, I had decided to leave and was walking across the highway when I spotted Wendy standing alone on the curb. At about the same time she spotted me and when I reached the curb she came running up and gave me a big hug. We chatted, excitedly, for about ten minutes. She had divorced her first husband and was remarried and had given birth, a while back, to her first child.

Shortly after we had started our conversation, a car pulled up, she smiled and gave me a second hug and then she climbed into that car and pulled away into the flow of traffic. I remember feeling so glad to see her but frustrated that the time we had was far too short.

A few years later at the tender age of twenty-six, her cancer re-emerged and it took her life swiftly and tragically. She was eight months pregnant, I believe, and was visiting her parents when she started to scream in pain. She was rushed to the hospital where they discovered she had developed brain tumors and was unable to safe her. God's blessing was that they were able to surgically remove the baby and save its life.

To this day, there are nights, when I wake up from a dream, staring at that empty spot in the palm of my hand where a dime used to reside. And a beautiful smile from that golden haired girl has left me again, with those unusual tingling sensations that I had first experienced when I was ten. And then I find myself feeling grateful for just having had the opportunity to have known her.

••••••••

Unlike a lot of families that are suddenly joined at the hip through marriage where the best outcome of that relationship is mere tolerance, my grandfather, grandmother, father and mother had a wonderful relationship. And one of their common interests that helped to bond that beautiful relationship was their love of the outdoors. My father grew up in northeast Wisconsin amongst the millions of acres of national forested land; where his father worked as a logger and a part-time farmer. Nine kids and two adults occupied a four-room log cabin with a huge roofed front porch and a two holed outhouse.

If you ever have had the opportunity to watch an episode of Little House on the Prairie where the children go to a one room school house and all of the grades are taught by one teacher, then you can imagine what it was like for my dad.

My father stated that they lived pretty much impoverished, but happy. He enjoyed living the life of a modern-day Davy Crockett, spending his days doing chores and then hunting, fishing or exploring the wilderness around the homestead. I can remember sitting spellbound, listening to the many stories he had to share about his encounters with the large, furry and dangerous animals they co-existed with on a daily basis. There was the time, when my grandmother had asked dad to go to the general store to pick up some milk. Now the main road was located one mile down the logging road where the cabin stood and the store another mile from that there.

After dad had purchased the milk, he decided that a short cut through the woods would save him some return time. Carrying the two one-gallon metal milk containers, one in each hand, he left the main road and headed off through the heavily forested woodlands.

Shortly, after entering the woods, the daylight faded and the shadows grew but because of his frequent forays, he was confident in finding his way home even in the darkening light.

When suddenly he heard the sound of feet shuffling through the leaf littered forest floor. Turning around, he shockingly discovered that a pack of wolves were moving directly towards him and closing the gap rather quickly. Dad stated that at that moment he really believed he was facing his young demise and with a burst of energy that only large amounts of adrenaline can provide, he started sprinting towards home.

As he ran, he saw a wolf matching him stride for stride on either side. With the rest of the pack close behind. Dad said he ran as if the fiery demons of hell were giving chase and the terror finally ended when he broke through the woods and entered the farm field that lay below cabin.

It was at that point in the story I would always ask dad why the wolves had not dragged him to the ground, and with fang and claw, tore him to bloody shreds. He would smile and then state matter of fact, he concluded that the wolves were not interested in his form of protein but rather they wanted the sweet, fat rich milk that he was carrying in those two metal containers. And if he had just dropped those milk containers, the harrowing chase would probably never have happened.

But his most common encounters were with the larger predators of northern Wisconsin, the black bear. Many a time walking to school a sow black bear would step out onto the road way, stand on her hind legs and bar their movement until her cubs had safely crossed the road. Or the times they would be trout fishing and get chased off of their favorite fishing hole by a bear that was cooling itself in the cold waters of the creek. He always reminded me that if you ever encounter a bear at close proximity do not turn and run. Because of their chase instinct it would engage their predator instinct. But instead, you needed to stand your ground and then slowly back away. A good rule of thumb that one day I would have to put to the test.

Now my grandfather had a great love for camping and fishing. I was camping long before I was even potty trained. Every summer weekend or weekly vacations, we were on the road to a distant campsite. And I fondly remember the many great times and wonderful experiences we had and the amazing people we met along the way.

It was that love of the outdoors that finally helped my grandfather make his decision to purchase the vacation cabin on Crooked Lake. We still did our camping trips every summer, but the cabin started to become the focal point for a lot of our gatherings.

We had a blast at that small cabin. Almost every weekend, it was packed to the rafters with friends, family and relatives enjoying the swimming, boating, card playing, fishing, horseshoes, campfires and overall camaraderie. We used to pack ourselves into the cars after dark and go to the garbage dump to watch the bears come out and feed; it was a Wisconsin form of Rocky Mountain High.

I remember the day of the bear attack as if it happened yesterday. It is amazing how the brain stores minute details of a traumatic event.

We got up to a gorgeous but hot and humid August day. It was still dark and when I opened my eyes, the smell of eggs, bacon, toast and coffee was filling the cabin. I could hear my dad bustling around the kitchen with the banging of pots and pans and the clinking of glasses and silverware as he prepared breakfast. Now most men can admit to cooking skills such as barbecuing hamburgers, hotdogs and brats, but my dad had a real knack for cooking and probably prepared more than half of our meals at home.

He also had a love for gardening and growing his own vegetables in our backyard which provided him considerable enjoyment. After harvest time, we would help in preparing them for canning or freezing, an art form that is rapidly diminishing in this country.

His favorite food was tomatoes. I witnessed my father slurp down half a ketchup bottle just to relish the tomato taste. He would grow all kinds of tomatoes in the garden and after a while, he discovered a small in-house variety that would grow and ripen throughout the winter.

But anyway, back to the story. After gulping down the wonderful morning meal, we grabbed our trout fishing gear and headed for the car. We talked excitedly about the upcoming fishing adventure and who was going to catch the biggest fish of the day. As we turned down the gravel road the sun was already a bright red spot on the distant horizon; the smell of pine trees filled the humid, hot summer morning and I was scanning the wood line for a glimpse of my favorite quarry, the whitetail deer.

Dad slowed the car and pulled over onto the shoulder of the road. We exited the vehicle and headed for the trunk of the car to extract our fishing gear. Now dad had the latest, greatest trout fishing gear. A dull green worm container hung from his belt. It had a rotating cover that allowed him to retrieve a night crawler when he needed one, my worm container was a small plastic box that was stuffed into a pocket of my jeans. He had rubber hip boots that insulated his legs from the clear, cold waters, for me it was my socks, tennis shoes and jeans as my only insulation. He wore a broad brimmed hat that protected his eyes from the glare of the sun. My thick head of light brown hair was my headgear. Even without all of the fancy fishing equipment, I enjoyed the days spent with my father chasing the elusive brook, brown and rainbow trout that inhabited the cold streams and creeks of northern Wisconsin.

This particular fishing hole required quite a walk. My dad always relished finding the hard-to-reach spots. This method usually guaranteed us very little fishing competition and a great chance at bagging our limit of delicious tasting trout.

We walked down through the pine trees for about a half a mile made a right turn at the bottom of a hill and walked another half mile until we reached the edge of the marsh. The deeply shaded pine groves gave way to bright sunshine when you entered the marsh. You could hear the gurgling of the creek, as it wound its way through the wetland. I could see the willows and alders that lined its bank about three hundred yards away. To reach it; I had to slug through a landscape filled with muck bottom potholes of knee-deep water, interspersed with tufts of bunchgrass. It was at this point that dad and I split up, he fished upstream and I would fish downstream. Dad gave me the usual good luck speech and headed along the edge of the marsh towards his designated fishing hole.

I, on the other hand, started to trudge through the marsh towards the creek that was straight ahead of my position. The walking was slow and tedious. You would step on top of a grassy tussock and your foot would slide down the edge into the cold, mucky water. And it seemed that for every three or four steps you took forward, you would end up falling backwards or forwards at least once into that cold, muddy water. I had approached to about one hundred yards of the creek when I heard a large splash. Because of the willows that grew along the creek bank it was difficult to see what was splashing in the creek, but I assumed it was another of the numerous beavers that inhabited such ecosystems so I continued to plod on.

After covering about another twenty yards, I heard a sound that made me stop dead in my tracks. Looking up I saw the head and the shoulders of a large black bear staring directly at me. The bear was growling and popping his teeth and I could tell by his demeanor that he was not at all happy with my presence. I remember standing knee deep in the black, mucky water of the marsh, staring at the bear as if a nightmare had suddenly become reality. Fear was gripping me as surely as a vice grips its intended work. The momentary pause of time, as the bear slowly eyed its intruder, was shattered by his dropping down on all fours and charging at me like a runaway locomotive. When he was about fifty yards away, he slammed on the brakes, reared up and continued his menacing behavior. He then dropped down on all four legs and would shake his head and shoulders back and forth. And suddenly with explosive acceleration, he charged. The second charge stopped as abruptly as the first. But this time he had closed the gap to about twenty yards away. I was standing there, frozen, unable to believe the reality that I was about to be severely mauled by a large and powerful bear.

After the same behavioral posturing, he dropped to the ground and charged me a third time. I can still see the bear, in my mind's eye, charging me, his narrow, black, beady eyes transfixed on me, the muddy stained marsh water was spraying up in great geysers with every step he took, and when it seemed that he was about to make contact, he slammed on the brakes so close to me, that I was instantly covered in the same mud stained water that the bear was displacing. As the bear reared up on its hind legs, I swore that his height blocked out the sun and those glistening, sharp teeth were as big as farming scythes.

In that split second between doom and destiny, the bear must have decided that the spindly twelve-year old boy standing frozen in fear before him was either to bony for a good meal or was not worth exerting any more energy in an already too hot August morning.

The bear then promptly dropped down on all fours and began to walk slowly back towards the bubbling brook. When he put another twenty yards between himself and I, the words of my father started screaming in my head. I began to slowly backup with shaky legs that, at times, seemed too weak and unstable to support my weight. I remembered what dad had said about his encounters with bears, so I purposely squashed the overwhelming desire to turn and run. I continued to walk slowly backwards, slipping and falling while keeping a sharp eye on the bruin.

Every so often the bear would stop and turn his head to keep an eye on my behavior and progress. It seemed like hours, but suddenly my last step put me on high ground. And after placing about twenty feet of pine trees between myself and the bear, I turned and ran so swiftly that my feet barely touched the ground, as if I was running on pure air. I remember that the fishing hook, that had been placed inside one of the rods eyes, suddenly broke free and quickly became snagged on a passing tree limb. I never stopped nor broke stride, I could hear the high-pitched whine of the fishing line as it was rapidly torn away from the spinning reel. And when I finally reached the end of the fishing line, it parted company from that reel with the sharp crack of a pistol shot. I do not remember most of the sprint back to the car, except for the overpowering fear that the bear had changed his decision for mercy and was now in hot pursuit to deliver his final verdict.

I do remember diving into the back seat of dad's car and slamming down the locks. Like a sudden, sweeping thunderstorm, the emotion from that close encounter burst forth in the form of screams, wails and weeping. I sat petrified and crying for hours until I saw my father walking towards the car. I burst forth from the back seat and threw myself into my father's arms crying uncontrollably.

After he was able to calm me down, I told him of the harrowing ordeal I had just encountered and he rocked me in his arms until I felt safe enough to leave the safety of his body.

The drive back to the cabin was rather quiet, I was exhausted from the adrenaline and the emotional energy of the ordeal, but I do remember my dad telling me how proud he was that I had done the right things and did not provoke the bear into finishing one of his charges. And that the bear was probably using that particular fishing hole to keep himself cool on that hot and humid August day.

The rest of the day is rather a blur in my memory. The encounter I had with that bear left no desire in me for trout fishing until I reached the age of seventeen. I would satisfy my fishing sweet tooth from the cushioned seat of a boat, set drifting lazily across the expanse of some Wisconsin lake, where the probability of meeting a black bear was about absolute zero.

For years I would occasionally have nightmares about being chased by bears. And as I got older, I came to realize that the bear was just protecting his natural cooling system from an unwelcome quest and that, in the end, I had the rare opportunity to experience nature on its own ground and on its own terms.

• • • • ••• •• • ••

I know most every town in the snow belt of America has that hill that is known for its perilous sledding capabilities. But Kaukauna had a hill that was notorious for chewing up kids, sleds and toboggans. It was well known that the local hospital was especially busy and where check-ins at its emergency room would suddenly spike, football season and sledding season.

This hill was located on the north side of town, right behind the famed Grignon (pronounced GREENO) home. The Grignon home was the oldest house in Kaukauna. It was built by a fur trader back in the day when only native Indians roamed and lived in the area. But by the time I hit the ground, it had long been turned into a museum. On a summer day, when the usual activities needed a rest, we hit our parents up for admission money and headed towards this famous landmark. It had a glass case that housed the rumored skeletal remains of several Indians that had been discovered on the property. I never believed the rumor, in my suspicious mind it was a red herring, a diversion from the truth. Those skeletal remains were actually kids, victims of Mount Misery. A grim reminder, a warning of its dangers and it wasn't long before I discovered its cruelty.

I was in seventh grade and had just started going to the new school called Quinney. It was built about five blocks from my house and was right on the edge of town. This is where I met my new friend Joe Jacobson. He lived on the north side of town and his parents ran the local pool hall. It was where I discovered French fries dipped in tartar sauce, pizza burgers and cherry cola. During our Christmas break that year, while spending a night at Joe's house, we hatched an ingenious idea on how to seriously maim ourselves.

It had been a great winter for sledding; the snow had started early and had come down in blissful white, crystalline drifts. We had spent the day sledding and tobogganing, a day full of adrenaline riddled excitement.

Mount Misery was long and steep, except for a little natural shelf located about one third of the way down. The runs were long and fast. Many a kid got plowed under from runaway sleds or toboggans. It was not unusual, when standing on the summit, to witness kids viciously thrown, helter-skelter, into the air on impact as if struck by a vehicle at high speed. Toboggans ferrying the injured and maimed flowed past in a constant stream.

[73]

Regardless of its dangers, kids flocked to its allure. It provided exceptional thrills only found at distant and expensive theme parks. On those nights when the snow felt soft and heavy, children, at times, would disappear into its white veil as if abducted by an alien force, only to reappear years later. Each run seemed to last forever and the return hike was akin to scaling mount Everest.

We were all in agreement that Mount Misery was the best doggone sledding hill in the Fox Valley. It is a common ritual when boys turn thirteen, they feel that a test of their manhood is somehow necessary, it is something akin to an Aborigine walkabout or a Cherokee rite of passage. We decided that the thrill of traveling at sixty miles an hour while shards of dry snowflakes imbedded painfully into our frozen faces was not quite up to snuff. Besides, in other cultures, boys who had turned our age were given rites of passage that were much more dangerous than sliding down a hill at auto racing speeds. For example, there were the ancient Antelope Valley Indians who hunted grizzly bears with nothing but a spear, talk about a true test of your manhood. I wonder how many never came home.

Anyway, after a long debate, we finally decided on our test of adolescent testosterone. We would build a ramp on the shelf of Mount Misery and if we constructed it high enough and strong enough, we might actually achieve near orbital altitude.

After a few phone calls, we gathered up enough of our friends to aid in our grand endeavor. The plan was to meet at Mount Misery, at night preferably, around nine o'clock when the winter temperatures would plummet into the sub-zero range.

With our little army of laborers, we quickly built the ramp out of packed snow. The ramp was about three feet wide, five feet high and curved upward to about a forty-five-degree angle, the perfect incline to provide maximum trajectory and distance. To finish the final phase of construction we needed to water down the ramp which would create a crust of slick ice, thus increasing our launch speed considerably. We formed an old-fashioned bucket brigade and with a helping house nearby, we completed the task with only a handful of frostbite injuries. After a careful last inspection; we headed home for a good night's sleep.

The next day dawned sunny and bright, perfect weather for a Cape Canaveral like liftoff. The launch would be executed at night thus allowing enough time for the adolescent news mill to rattle around and generate the kind of crowd we desired.

[74]

As the last rays of the winter sun were beginning to retreat towards the equator, we bundled up into our layers of winter clothing and began the trek towards Mount Misery and the sledding event that awaited us.

As we neared Mount Misery, we realized our marketing move was successful. Scores of kids turned out to witness the event, and as we approached the launch site, dragging our three-man toboggan behind us, a cheer suddenly erupted from the crowd. We became instant celebrities and not wanting to waste the moment, we turned towards the crowd and greeted our admirers enthusiastically.

Reaching our starting point, we felt the tension increase dramatically, kids were talking loudly and excitedly and I swear I could hear some kids taking bets on our success or failure. Like insects drawn to a light, people are drawn to potential disasters. Scores of people attend a NASCAR event just in the hopes of seeing cars disintegrate when slamming into a wall at two hundred miles an hour when life and limb is on the line. And for us it was no different.

We quickly began our pre-flight check list, was the toboggan properly waxed, check. Was the approach ramp properly aligned, check. Did we have the necessary equipment, hats, boots, jackets, and gloves, check. The time had come, I could feel the exhilarating rush of adrenaline, a dry mouth and a racing heart, while my respirations had dramatically increased. One by one we climbed into our predefined seating arrangements, Joe up front, me in the middle, Kurt, Joe's brother, in the rear of the toboggan.

The winter night suddenly fell into focus. I felt the cold air against my cheeks as we settled into our seating positions. Just before launch, there was an unexpected moment of quiet anticipation and then with a shout, the runner began to push us down the snow packed course.

We picked up speed with amazing quickness, the first possible catastrophe was staring us in the eye. If we veered off course and if Kurt was unable to correct in time, we would impact the ramp with only half of the toboggan resulting in a dangerous barrel roll and a bone crushing impact.

As we closed in on the ramp, at ever increasing speed, we were relieved to find ourselves right on track. We hit the ramp at about thirty to forty miles per hour and launched off in a perfect forty-five-degree trajectory. I saw the ground quickly disappear from view while the night sky loomed into sight.

The stars twinkled with an absolute brilliance; the wind whistled while the biting air felt like bee stings upon my face. And for a brief moment, I felt I could reach out and touch those heavenly lights.

At this point we had reached about ten feet of altitude. And as the toboggan began to shed velocity and as gravity began to pull us downward, I felt a momentary experience of weightlessness, as if I was strapped into a Mercury Seven rocket as it broke through earth's atmosphere. As we passed over the pinnacle of our trajectory, the toboggan began to nose down towards the snow-covered ground below.

As the slope of Mount Misery began to rapidly rise up, an uncomfortable feeling began to gnaw in the pit of my stomach. We were approaching touchdown, not at a dangerous angle, but with way too much speed. The toboggan hit lightly front first and then slammed into the landing zone with incredible force. The toboggan immediately broke up and Joe, Kurt and I were thrown clear of the sled. I hit the ground hard, and the world instantly turned black and I felt the horrible sensation of collapsed lungs.

Soon after my vision returned and I was able to refill my lungs, the pain at the top of my butt became severe and unbearable. As I looked around, kids were running down the slope and soon we were surrounded by friends and strangers alike. The lists of injuries were as follows, Joe broke his left arm, Kurt broke his right arm and I fractured my tail bone. But the praise and the admiration we received was awesome. For a brief moment in time, we had achieved local fame and glory.

Looking back, it was probably one of the most ignorant decisions I have ever made. The results could have been much more disastrous and life changing. And, to be completely honest, I did not feel that manhood was any closer than it was before I performed that dangerous stunt. I guess manhood is not just a matter of proving one's courage, but rather manhood is defined throughout one's life time. It's tested each time life rears up and challenges our character and our values. It is honed when we make good, moral decisions and accept the personal responsibility of those decisions. The lesson I learned that cold, painful night at Mount Misery was much more valuable than obtaining peer-based fame and glory it helped me to realize what is truly the test of our manhood.

• • •• • • •• •• • •• •

As a teenager, one of the many fun filled activities during the summer was to go skinny dipping. We would gather a group of friends and in the darkness of the night, take off our clothes and swim, naked. There are specific words attached to skinny dipping moves. For example, if dive under water, resurface and then dive back under water, and if leave your bare butt exposed for a brief period of time where the soft light of the moon reflects off the smooth, white surface, this is called doing a porpoise. Those late-night events were usually held at abandoned quarries or at one of our numerous lakes

It was a beautiful summer night in Wisconsin, the day was hot, humidity so thick you could cut it with a knife. The nights provided little relief from the sweltering temperatures. Most homes were devoid of central air conditioning and even with the windows and doors wide open, relief was scarce. It was during these scorching times that skinny dipping, especially late at night, was ever so popular.

That hot summer night Ray Kappell and I had decided it was time to make a run to Lower Cliff State Park and immerse ourselves into the cool, algae bloomed waters of Lake Winnebago.

Upon arrival, we found the front gate chained and padlocked. The park closed at ten pm, for a pair of overheated teenage boys, it was just a suggestion. Pulling the truck over onto the grassy shoulder, we proceeded to dispose of our valuables, wallets and shoes. And then with great anticipation, we climbed the fence and proceeded to walk towards the closed beach.

Upon arrival we found a small mix of boys and girls, swimming, laughing and having a good time. The cool waters of the lake felt sensational and it wasn't long before the," I dare you", challenges were cast and in the blink of an eye, there we were, skinny dipping.

The dimly lit curtain of the night mostly obscured our naked bodies except for the occasional white as snow buttock rose up out of the lakes opaque surface. Ray and I had swum farther out into the lake than the rest of the kids when, without warning, out the darkness there appeared bright lights and harsh voices commanding kids to vacate the water.

In that moment of panic girls cried and pleaded for their clothes while the park rangers demanded an immediate exit. Quickly, Ray and I, outside of the beams of their flashlights, decided to evade the trespassing net. Without a sound, we slipped below the dark surface of the lake and swam parallel to the shore and away from the park rangers.

As Ray and I put more distance between us and the agitated park rangers, we realized our escape went unnoticed and it left us with a sense of relief as we giggled and talked in hush tones.

We swam quietly underwater with the occasional surfacing for about three hundred more yards and then quietly exited the lake. We could still vaguely hear the excited voices of the kids and park rangers as they placed those kids under arrest. We had one problem; our clothes which consisted of denim shorts and a T-shirt, were being confiscated by the authorities which left us with wearing only our birthday suits.

As we crossed the large expanse of a field while running naked, it felt like every eye in the area were gawking at us. Once we reached the truck, Ray fired up the engine and drive us back home.

I don't believe the word awkward best describes the feeling when two completely naked boys are beating a hasty retreat in his friend's father's truck. I remember repeating the mantra over and over, please don't get pulled over for speeding, I don't quite know how to explain, to the officer, why we were wearing the king's invisible clothes.

After a tense twenty-minute drive we arrived at Ray's house, thank goodness the house was empty. We parked the truck in the dark garage and then sprinted into his house. After scrounging through his dresser, for clothes, we headed downstairs, cracked open a beer and laughed until our ribs ached.

Did this encounter discourage any future episodes of skinny dipping, well no, we just decided to stay out of State Parks after closing hours. There was this later incident that involved, skinny dipping and forty-five-degree water but that is for another story.

• • • •• • • •• • •

Regrets, regrets, everyone has their fair share of regrets. The girl you never asked to the dance, the job opportunity you didn't take. Regrets by its very definition are personal significant points in our lives that help to define our weaknesses, our inability to leap outside of our comfort zone. Fueled by our fears and inadequacies. The interesting aspect of regrets is they don't become regrets until the passage of time, the accumulation of wisdom and of course that valuable little nugget called 20/20 hindsight. But sometimes that regret can propel you to make a change and that change can help to make you a better person.

A child's world can be a magical place, where imaginations are developed and nurtured, a stick removed from a tree by a strong autumn wind, becomes the sword that slays the dragon and frees the beautiful princess or the smooth round stone found by the gurgling stream becomes the weapon with which you slay the dreaded giant. But it can also be a cruel and demeaning place. Children born with physical handicaps are, at times, mercilessly picked upon. Pummeled by the jeers and taunts from others erodes their already fragile self-esteem as surely as water dissolves a rock over time.

This story is not going to be written in a humorous manner, for what we did was not funny nor humorous at all, but I hope you would lean an important lesson in dealing with others, not as fortunate as ourselves, in a more kind and humane manner.

There was a boy, I can't remember his name, so I will give him a story name of Bill, he lived at the end of 18th street. And during the summer it was not uncommon for my friends and myself to be sitting on my dad's front porch discussing or planning our day's activities. At times, he would suddenly appear and within our presence, sit down on the sidewalk and play a coffee can as if it were a bongo drum while singing horribly out of tune.

He had Down syndrome, where a child is born having an extra chromosome, no fault of their own, just a bad break. In our day we called those types of people retards and during those encounters, we would mock him and say mean and cruel things, at times he would cry. At other times, he would yell at us but that was just met with more jeers and more taunts. Leaving, he hung his head and walked away.

As children you always seem to live in the moment, never pondering the consequences of your actions. Well, our day of reckoning was bearing down upon us. We were blissfully unaware of it, until a Saturday morning.

That summer morning dawned bright, sunny and warm, the perfect day to spend at one of our favorite childhood haunts, a place called Butter clay.

Butter clay was located about three quarters of a mile from 18th street. We would walk to the end of 18th street take a right onto Oakridge Drive and then a left on 20th street. Walk between two houses and head down the hill to the railroad tracks. Once on the railroad tracks, we would walk about a good five city blocks and cross the old barbed wire fence and viola, you were there.

Butter Clay was a unique place; the creek lazily meandered around a wooded lot passing by a huge tree that overhung the creek bank. At the base of that tree was a small cave, created by years of spring floods and summer gully washers. We would crawl into that cave, and dig for Indian arrow heads or just to get away from the summer heat and humidity.

That Saturday morning, we spent our time sliding down the smooth clay banks into the refreshing water of the creek. It had rained the day before and those clay banks were wet and very slick. After a few hours of sliding and swimming, we climbed out of the creek and sat, relaxing, at the top of the bank. Suddenly, Norman and I spotted Bill as he walked down the railroad tracks carrying an unidentified object in his hands.

When he was parallel to us and about twenty yards away, I realized, with dread, that that object in his hands was a twelve-gauge pump shotgun. I watched, in shock, as he slowly raised the weapon and pointed it at us. Norman and I gave a shrill cry for everyone to take cover. while Norman and I ran to the back of the big tree. Peering around the tree, I saw that our friends were diving and sliding over and down the bank of the creek when without warning, the first shotgun blast peppered the front of the large tree we were hiding behind. Standing behind the protective cover of the tree, my body shook, as he unloaded five shotgun rounds at us, fortunately none of those lethal pellets had found their mark. After a moment of silence, I chanced a peek and I saw that he just kept racking the pump and pulling the trigger not realizing the gun was empty. Our blessing was that he had not brought any additional ammunition.

After a few minutes he slowly lowered the weapon, turned and walked away. It was then that I left the safety of the tree as we gathered together to make sure none of us were in any serious medical condition.

After our initial fright we became very angry and started following him home pummeling him with stones and BBs from our BB guns. Once we got to the top of 20th street, we made a beeline for the Sheriffs house just down the block. He was home and after calming us down, he was able to get an accurate account of what had taken place. I don't know what happened to Bill, I really don't recall ever seeing him again. But as I got older and as I would revisit that incident, it became more and more apparent that our jeering and taunting had a direct effect on what he attempted to do to us that summer morning. In my teen years I became more tolerant of those people who were different and less tolerant to those who would jeer and taunt them.

Sometimes I wonder how different that day would have been and how different his circumstances would have been if instead of mocking him, we would have befriended him.

• • •• •• • ••• • • • •• • • •

I was in my deer stand this morning, a beautiful fall day, leaves displayed in their brilliant colors, squirrels scampering through the fallen vestiges looking for breakfast, when a wave of reminiscence swept over me, a memory flashed into my mind, a memory forty-nine years old. It was 1967, I was a skinny blonde haired twelve-year old boy, the Beatles had released their Sgt Pepper's album and it was the summer of love.

A family friend Bud Parker, for reasons unknown, had taken a shine to me when I was but a six-year-old, snot nosed kid; he had remarked, years later, he almost passed up renting my father's upstairs apartment because he spied my snot nose pressed up tight against the window. He became more than a tenant to my family, he became a great family friend and my mentor, especially in the budding art of Archery,

I remember the day, I was six, when he walked me down the store's aisle, we stopped in front of the archery display. I saw bows crafted of wood and fiberglass; my heart beat fast as he asked me to choose. I picked the yellow fiberglass with the black handle, a ten-pound draw beauty, along with the accessories, an arm guard, a shooting glove and six matching wooden arrows. He had bought me my first bow, instructed me in the ancient art of its use and developed in me a passion that lasted a lifetime.

Fast forward six years, I am now 12, and quite proficient with a bow. The Christmas before, I received an upgrade, a Bear Cub recurve in thirty-two-pound draw and a dozen wooden arrows, six bristling a razor sharp broadhead and six with field points for practice.

Early in September, I walked the eight blocks to the local hardware store and purchased my first ever deer hunting license. I had never been so excited. I had spent the previous year's honing my skill on paper targets and the overabundance of chipmunks at my grandparent's cottage. With my newly acquired archery license neatly tucked away in my blue jeans, I was ready. The next weekend, Bud drove us out of town to a place that he had recently acquired permission to hunt. It was my first archery hunt and upon arrival to our destination, we grabbed our equipment and began the walk across a small grassy field. At the wood line we entered a low area filled with yellow marsh grass that swayed in the gentle breeze. It was surrounded by an area of new timber growth and mature hard woods. It was here Bud stopped and looked down at me, with a smile, he quickly analyzed my hunting attire which consisted of blue jeans and a dark shirt. With a chuckle, "Bob having no hat and with your blonde hair I am going to sit you down in the march grass, you should perfectly blend in here".

As he walked away from my appointed ambush location, I proceeded to mat down the stalks of marsh grass until I had formed a small circle, with no seat upon which to sit, I knelt down into the soft soil and began my patient vigilance. The warm fall sun, caressing my face, had made me sleepy and as my head slowly descended towards my chest, I suddenly heard the sound of feet quickly approaching my position. In front of me, 15 yards away, was a barbed wire fence, that separated the marsh grass from the woods. To my right the woods extended well beyond. A doe first appeared bounding easily through the grass followed closely by a buck. I raised up out the yellow grass, pulled the string back and followed that buck until he disappeared from sight. That's right, I never released the arrow, my heart seemed like it was going to pound out of my chest, my entire body was shaking. I sat back down in the grass confused and disappointed, attempting to collect myself while berating myself for not releasing the arrow. Suddenly, ten deer appeared in the woodlot in front of me and on the opposite side of the barbed wire fence, my body trembled as I stood up, took careful aim and then sat back down, I repeated that procedure three times before the deer had had enough of my humorous display and bounded untouched away, their white tails waving me goodbye.

As tears filled my eyes, I sat down feeling worthless and dejected. I couldn't understand why I had not fired a single arrow, all those years of preparation and I froze. In that moment, I was never more disgusted with myself.

After dark Bud came out and, in my anguish, I told him my story Expecting a brow beating for my poor performance, I was instead surprised when he laughed and tousled my hair. He looked me in the eye and said welcome to the wonderful world of bow hunting. That day fired up a passion inside of me that still burns bright today, thanks Bud.

• • •• ••• ••• • • • • •• • • •

Now that I am over sixty-five-years old, I love to reflect back upon the rigors and trials of my youth, those days are perfectly and stubbornly planted into my memory until, I hope not, they become the last vestiges of Alzheimer's. These moments frozen in time are as warming as a fire on a cold winter's day and as comforting as the embrace of a loved one. Here is one of those moments, my first puppy love.

The snow fell softly as we left the Friday night dance. The cold air felt good, upon our sweat induced bodies, as the crystallized snow crunched faintly under our footsteps. The Beatles song "Hey Jude" was still ringing in my ears as she suddenly, but gently slipped her hand into mine. We walked silently for a while taking in the beauty of the pristine snow as it draped itself upon the hedges and piled up, in a blanket of white, upon the yards and the empty streets. It glittered as fields of sparkling diamonds, under the soft light of the street lamps.

Kathy Hooyman, Pinky as she was called, and I had been dating for about three weeks. She was a friend of my older sister Gail and we had met because of that friendship. She was one year older than I and our relationship started as so many young infatuations that consisted of awkward conversations that morphed into moments much more comfortable.

At our first school dance together it was the usual, the boys plastered against the gym walls, stealing glimpses of the young ladies, standing in circles and talking excitedly.

As the music filled the gymnasium, the girls gathered themselves upon the dance floor while the boys struggled to gather their courage. Because I, being the only boy in the family and being raised with three sisters, had the rare opportunity to learn the most current dances of the day. My older sister would spin a platter and grab me, mostly grumbling from the couch and have me be her dance partner. At the time, it was a mix of annoyance and fun as long as none of my buddy's caught me in the act.

But karma has a way of enhancing those experiences, it provided me with the confidence, early on, to dance with my sweetheart, while others stood and stared.

At first, fast songs, stirred up the audience as they swayed and bounced to the beat, whipping us into a musical frenzy. And later on, as the lights dimmed, we danced slowly, our bodies touching, hands

[84]

clasped, with heads laid upon shoulders. It was a magical time. For many of us, the first experience in the realm of relationships. It was a confusing and exciting time.

After the dance, it was the walk, mostly spent in silence, but enveloped in a feeling of closeness. We made our way from the dance through the glistening snow. And stopped in front of the grocery store, close to her home. Turning our faces towards each other, we softly held hands and talked in nervous tones, both attempting to summon the courage for what was expected next.

And then it happened, slowly tilting our heads, our lips met as the snow piled softly upon our shoulders. That moment seemed to have lasted a blissful eternity.

When our lips parted, I looked warmly into her eyes and smiled. Giving her a tight hug I watched her walk slowly away. She turned back, smiled and waved. I really don't remember the long walk home that cold, snow filled night, I was consumed with those first feelings and thoughts, confused but satisfying. It was my first real kiss.

But unfortunately, first loves don't last, just before her graduation of eight grade, she broke up with me, leaving my friendship ring and a letter upon my home room desk. I understood her reasoning; she was now a freshman in high school while I was still an eighth grader. It really was asking a little too much from the relationship.

But I will forever appreciate her companionship and her providing me my first kiss. I was heartbroken the following year when I heard the tragic news that she had died in a house fire along with some of her siblings and her mother, only her older brother and father had escaped the tragedy. That moment in time is forever etched upon my heart and so is her memory. Thanks Pinky.

• • • •• • • •• •• • • •

As the warmth of summer began to wane and gave way to the cool mornings of autumn, the blossoms of spring matured. Those delicious temptations always seem to invoke some minor criminal activity, especially in young boys. There was an older two-story house located across the parking lot from Dick's Drive In. An older house wrapped in white, with smudged windows that looked out upon Main Street and the small orchard that resided in its expansive backyard. it was a temptation to seductive to resist.

Growing up on 18th street was thrilling and adventurous My friends and co-conspirators were always coming up with new adventures and daring exploits. From the five-acre fire, to the underground forts, each new day was a thrilling new chapter in mischievousness and exciting exploits.

From the summer backyard campouts where, in the wee hours of the morning, as ghostly ninjas, we roamed other neighborhoods, looking for unsuspecting campers. Kids like us, enjoying a night of camaraderie. Sneaking as silent as the night, we removed tent stakes and then watched, with glee, as their canvass abode fell down around them.

To the street baseball games that, at times, ended with broken windows or limping home after a bruising backyard football game. Those were marvelous days, full of innocence without the distraction of digital devices and internet labyrinths But, in the fall, when blossoms turned into apples, we struck with reckless abandon.

The keeper of those marvelous fruit trees was an elderly woman, quiet and shy, we rarely saw her out and about. She existed in childhood myths and rumors, a mystery, as the rumor insisted, that spoke in broken English with a thick accent. It was the summer of our twelfth-year, the summer when the myth became a reality.

On a warm fall evening, after our normal activities such as ringing doorbells and tying Marks younger brother up and leaving him on the neighbor's porch. We sat quietly, on Marks side porch, enjoying the local cuisine, a pizza. When someone's thought slipped out, such an unexpected and accidental communication usually meant trouble. But it was out and we latched onto it like a tick on a hound. The thought went as follows, "boy an apple right now would sure hit the spot". Nothing elaborate nor profound, remember we were just twelve. But as sure as a lightning rod attracts a storms power, we were all in.

We spent the better part of the evening discussing our plan on how to successfully extract some delicious apples without alerting the mysterious lady or worse yet, the law. Even though our parents usually had a store-bought plastic bag full of such fruit, it was the adrenaline rush of sneaking in, undetected, and making off with the prize. I would bet, if properly studied, it was the probable influence of tv westerns that permeated the air waves in those days. Every Saturday as we sat cross legged on the floor, with our vision intensely focused, we watched as cowboys, in their western garb, snuck up on a war party of Indians, or a band of outlaws, slipped in unnoticed, and successfully regained their stolen horses or a chest full of gold. In our twelve-year-old world, it was the closest thing to nirvana.

We decided when the sun had finally slipped-into its nightly berth and darkness had descended upon the land, we would gather our forces and execute our carefully laid out plan. Our strategy was flawless, in a series of rock, paper, scissors the lucky winner was chosen to assault the objective, alone, as we hid at a safe distance, and return to the rest of us, one delicious Gala apple.

The mission was carried out in true military style. At the appointed time of departure, our hearts raced as we watched, the chosen one, with dirt hastily smeared upon his face, cautiously approach the base of the apple tree. Lying low upon the ground, we watched, anxiously, as he listened for any sounds that might alert us to danger. Crouching low he closed the distance and with a final surge, he made it to the objective. Carefully he climbed, but a misstep and a branch snapped and fell to the ground. Our hearts momentarily stopped as we waited for a response, for now, the coast was clear.

Licking our lips, we watched in anticipation as the chosen one, having tucked his shirt into his pants, filled that void with the objects of our desire.

As the mission was nearing its completion and our attention was waning, we unexpectedly caught movement.

Out the darkness, the mystery lady, slightly hunched over, wearing a knee length dress, with her white hair pulled back, tight, into bun, burst forth brandishing a weapon.

Before we had time to alert the chosen one, she descended upon him like the Mongol horde. With lightning-fast reflexes; the lady of rumors, using her weapon of choice, a straw broom, was beating the hell out of him. His only escape was to free fall onto the ground, disregard the bounty and run as if Satan himself was hot on his heels.

[87]

The next day as we were sitting on the picnic tables behind Dick's Drive In, licking our wounded egos, the mystery lady approached and gently lectured us on the dangers of climbing her apple trees. She explained, when a limb is broken, it no longer produces fruit and the more limbs we broke the less productive the tree. She had no problem with us picking any low hanging apples or even the ones that fell to the ground. After a round of yes ma'am's, she quietly left us to ponder her advice. Damn, once we had her permission to pick apples, the luster of that criminal activity just fell away. It no longer held any real interest.

As I got older and at times, while walking to high school, I would take the shortcut through her backyard and grab a delicious apple for breakfast. But for one night, we felt like buccaneer's sailing upon the high seas, looking for a majesties ship to plunder. Besides, intel had informed us of pear tree just up the street, ready for the taking.

• • • •• • • •• • • •• •• •• •• • •

The summers from around 1970 to 1973 were the best summers of my life and one of the reasons for this boast was of course the Kappell residence. Raymond's parents had recently purchased a cottage in northern Wisconsin and not wanting to miss enjoying their new acquisition, would spend many a weekend on its clear pristine waters surrounded by ancient boreal forests. Now I don't know if Ray's parents were simply naïve to our teenage intentions or were in fact, just turning a blind eye. But I know that some very special moments and events occurred at that address located at the top of Beaulieu Hill.

I received the call from Ray stating that his parents had just left for their vacation premises and, before their car had exited Beaulieu Hill, could I come over and help with the party plans. I grabbed my keys to the 63-ford galaxy and hollered some unintelligible phrase towards my dad as I vaulted out the back door.

Cranking up the V-8, I began daydreaming about the possible shenanigans and adventures this gala might provide, let's see, plenty of cold, frosty beer and plenty of tight jeaned, bobby socked beauties, oh ya, it was going to be a grand night. Looking into the rear-view mirror, and with a head full of expectation, I backed out and headed towards adventure.

Passing Dicks Drive In, I rolled the driver's window down and let the fresh air sweep through the car. Fumbling with the radio dial, I finally found a rock and roll radio station as the sweet and amazing guitar of Jimmy Hendricks broke through loud and clear. Driving north on Crooks Avenue, I made the right turn past the old Kaukauna Club Cheese Factory onto Dodge Street and as the V8 growled, I headed for Beaulieu Hill.

The cigarette smoke hung heavy in the car as I turned right onto Hill Crest Drive. Pressing down hard on the accelerator the car accelerated as it climbed the steep incline. Looking out of the passenger window, I watched the younger kids as they played and splashed in the city pool.

After negotiating the dangerous S turns at the top of the hill, I finally arrived at Ray's house and pulled onto the grey stained driveway. Turning off the ignition, I felt the engine cough and sputter a few times and as I exited the old Ford, I thought to myself, man I needed to get that damn carburetor fixed. Entering into the back of the house, the door creaked loudly on its rusted hinges signaling my entrance.

I saw Ray standing in the kitchen talking to Pat. As I walked into the room, we high fived each other and then quickly began to discuss the pre party plans. Ray would take the truck and fetch the night's alcoholic refreshments while Pat and I held down the fort just in case people began to arrive ahead of schedule.

After what seemed like an eternity, I heard the sound of a Rays truck as it pulled onto the driveway. Looking out of the smeared kitchen window, I saw Ray and a stranger exit the truck. I turned to Pat and asked "who the hell is that".

As Ray and the stranger entered the kitchen, Pat and I exchanged puzzled looks. Ray smiled and explained he saw the kid hitch hiking and decided what the hell and gave him a lift. Ray, being the friendly personality he is, offered him an invitation. The stranger accepted.

After Ray left to retrieve the barrel full of tonight's foolishness, Pat and I started throwing questions at the stranger. During the questioning, he made a statement that hung suspended in the air like the strong pungent smell of cooked liver and onions, not believing what we heard, Pat and I asked him to repeat what he had just said, his unusual response, he was a circus performer. We stood dumbfounded, staring, as if he had just grown a second head. I then heard myself mutter something like, "what did you do in the circus". His next answer was even more bizarre. "I eat glass". Pat says, "no way", he says "yes I did", I say "no way", he says "yes I did".

Ray now back in the house is inquisitive, he sees the astonished look upon our faces. He says, "what's up", Pat responds, "He's a circus performer". Ray says, "no way", I say, "yep". What does he do Ray asks, "he eats glass", Pat replies. "No way", Ray says. "O hell ya", I reply. Ray turns and stares at the stranger. "Is that true", he asks. "Yup", responds the stranger.

Did you ever make a dare and then wish you could take it back? What happens next still makes me shiver and cringe.

Pat, wearing a smirk, says to the stranger "here's a beer glass, eat it". The stranger eyes the beer glass, picks it up and without concern, looks at Pat, at Ray and at me and takes a big ole bite.

At this point my knees are starting to knock and my butt is definitely puckering up; I slowly look at Ray and then at Pat and sure has hell, they have the same astonished look on their faces. The stranger chews and then swallows it. My brain is screaming please stop, I really don't want to see rivulets of blood running down your chin and gathering upon the floor in a crimson pool. But without hesitation, he takes his next bite, and chews it into sharp little pieces, the silence in the room was deafening,

I believe we all were waiting for the horror, but as he chewed each piece and then swallowed, it became apparent that our worse fears were not going to appear. After he swallowed the last piece of beer glass, we erupted in a cheer as if he had just kicked the field goal to win the super bowl. And if that wasn't bad enough, we asked him what other super powers of digestion did he possess, his answer, "I can eat roofing tacks on pizza". I looked at Ray and without saying a word Ray said "let me look and see if my dad has any of those in the garage". As Ray searched for the box of roofing tacks, Pat was now putting the grocery store cheese and sausage pizza in the oven. As we waited for the oven timer to tickle our ears, I kept watching him to see if any of that broken glass was attempting to make an early exit. I was staring so intensely that the oven alarm actually startled me and without hesitation he loaded the top of that hot, gooey, store-bought pizza with a handful of sharp roofing tacks and then seemingly with relish, began to devour that pizza, slice by tack filled slice.

The bile in my stomach was now attempting to climb my esophagus, as I was thinking, *"come on man no one can eat broken glass and a medium pizza loaded with roofing tacks and not hit the floor writhing in intestinal agony"*, I was getting scared, thoughts started to race through my mind, bad thoughts, like what are we going to tell the authorities why this man is lying in a large red pool of rectal blood, suddenly the stranger asks for something very peculiar to wash down his intestinal shredding meal, I couldn't believe what I heard, it wasn't a request for water or beer or wine or soda, he wanted to wash that meal down with a pint of brake fluid.

Now at this point any rational person would have said alright that's enough insanity for an evening, but no, Ray said, "wait I'll be right back" and within a short space there he was standing with a full pint of brake fluid. The man unscrews the cap, breaks the metallic cover and after a brief gesture of prost, he tips his head back and guzzles the whole pint of brake fluid. Now at this point I am starting to freak out, I pull Ray and Pat onto the back porch where we concoct our collaborative story for the authorities, even though this was all voluntary on the stranger's part and he wasn't coerced at any time in this bizarre display, we decided we needed to get him out of the house and to the emergency room.

As we re-entered the house to escort him to the nearest operating room, we suddenly discovered the stranger was now absent. Now becoming quite concerned, we began a search of the house, hopefully not for his corpse, when we heard the window break in the downstairs bathroom, damn I thought, is he going to try and eat that too.

Rushing to the bathroom door we quickly opened the portal expecting to see a bloody, writhing mass on the bathroom floor, instead we saw a shattered bathroom window with the curtains blowing softly to the rhythm of the breeze. Retreating back to the kitchen, we sat down and had a round of cigarettes and beer, incredibly recanting what we had just witnessed. After a sweep of the grounds around the house, we were assured that the stranger was indeed gone and had not expired from his bizarre meal.

To be honest I don't recall the rest of the night, we undoubtedly had another successful party at the Kappell house, but after you have actually been on an episode of the twilight zone everything else dims in comparison.

• • • •• • • •• •• • • •

The nights darkness clung desperately to the room, only the occasional intrusion of light from a passing car dared to interrupt its bleak purpose The photo book now lay upon my lap, turned to its last page of photogenic memory. I could taste the salty tear that clung to the corner of my mouth. The day had begun as a celebration, my baby, my last-born son had just finished his collegiate journey and with his freshly printed diploma in hand, he announced that the company he had worked for, as a co-op, had given him an offer of employment.

As I stared out the darkened window, a breath of night air softly brushed against my face and in that moment, as if transported by a cerebral magic carpet, I saw my wife standing in front of our full-length mirror, gently turning her head from side to side as she gazed expectantly at the miraculous belly bulge that was soon to be our third son. I affectionately wrapped my arms around that soft taunt human den and softly kissed her neck, placing my head against the side of her face and we both stared with wonder at that blessed bundle of life. We found ourselves smiling, encapsulated within its great expectation.

At the next breath of night air, I saw the chaos of the birthing room, filled with many sounds, sounds out of harmony, the mechanical whirrs and chirps of medical devices, the sound of human voices blending in and out as each one performed their birthing tasks, mingled with the loud grunts and groans as my wife worked feverishly to bring that new life into this world.

I took my designated room position, at that moment in time, an onlooker, an outsider, feeling absolutely helpless to attend to my wife's needs, while my constant companions, joy and fear, pitched a fierce battle. And then amidst the raucous din, a moment of silence, as our son made his worldly appearance, sliding effortlessly into the sure hands of our doctor.

As he lied upon my wife's bosom, a tremendous feeling of relief and joy was expressed in the volume of tears that rolled down our faces. I gently rubbed his tiny back and silently counted his fingers and toes, some traditions, even though archaic, are still stubbornly clung to.

As the images of those memories slowly faded, it was replaced by the sound of laughter, the beautiful tinkling of a child's voice, filling the spaces of my mind, the sound of plastic big wheels rubbing against a concrete surface, signaled the approach of a toddler's caravan, cheerfully chasing each other. His blonde hair, thick and wild blowing in the breeze, wearing the smile of enjoyment.

As father time wind down the day to evening, he would climb upon my warm lap and lay his sleepy head upon my chest, and listen to make sure the heart within my chest still beat its rhythmic harmony. While I gently massaged the top of his wispy, blonde head, I would silently pray, hoping this magical moment would never end.

As the next memory swirled, I saw a child standing at the front door, wearing crisp new school clothes and a bright blue backpack. I remember his nervous smile as the flash of the camera captured this monumental first, each of us excited and scared, him not knowing what to expect, me not being able to help. As he walked to the bus stop, I stood stoic in my pride and as the tears rolled slowly down my face, saddened that his early childhood would forever be lost.

As the seasons unfolded before my eyes, flickers of colored and vague pictures rolled past as if captured in time lapse. I saw him standing in his newly pressed suit, smelling of his father's cologne, clutching a brightly colored corsage, I also glimpsed the times spent in tears and joy as he sojourned through the maze of early loves and loves lost.

As the window curtained again fluttered and danced to the tune of the night breeze, there he was, standing, adorned in the honored colors of his alma mater, awaiting the metallic sound of his broadcasted name, to ascend the last steps of his academic journey and to grasp its golden award. I felt that same pride, my heart swelled, joy expressed in tears, a sense of awe. As if gazing through life's kaleidoscope, the images began melding into and out of each other, each one familiar but unique, each one lovingly wrapped within segments of my life, pieces of me forever attached.

This is not the story of one son, but all of my sons, each one a blessing each one as unique as a snow flake, each one's leaving the nest was mingled with the feeling of parental pride and heartbreak. And as the last child left the nest, the silence it left, was deafening.

• • •• ••• ••• ••• •• • •• • • • •

As a kid, around fourteen, life starts to take on just a wee bit more complexity, why you ask, because that hormonal change called puberty is about to hit you like a Mac Truck.

The golden sunset draped itself across the landscape signaling the end of another stunning summer day. As I sat upon the warm, weathered, concrete front porch, I pondered the day's activities already spent, swimming at the city pool, exploring the beauty and the secrets of the nearby woods and playing a game called the fox and the hounds, a game requiring copious amounts of energy and summer time sweat.

As the sun set deeper into the horizon, the nights shadows began to creep silently, replacing the fading light. From the living room, I could smell the tantalizing aroma of my dad's roast beef, baked potatoes and percolating coffee. Soon, I was hovering over the steaming and gurgling pots and pans, impatiently awaiting their arrival. "Wow, pops that sure does smell good" I said with a grin. Holding a wooden ladle in his hand, he lowered his head and looked through his brushy eyebrows and exclaimed, "bob, please don't hover over the stove, I don't need any hair spoiling my dinner, and by the way, you can make yourself useful by setting the table". "Sounds good to me pops", I replied, as I spun around and gathered up the essential utensils and proceeded to set them in their proper placements.

Dad walked to the bottom of the stairs and hollered, "girls suppers ready" and within seconds the sound of stampeding feet echoed and reverberated through the house. In these moments, if one was not quick of feet, serious injury was a good possibility.

As we gathered at our places around the table, with the plethora of delicious foods awaiting our consumption, dad picked one of us to say grace. "Bob how about you say grace tonight". Lowering my head, to a more reverent position, and folding my hands, I began my prayer, "rub a dub dub, thanks for the grub, yah God, yah God", Dad looked up and without saying a word, worked me over with his you better get serious right quick look. Wiping the grin off my face, I began again, "bless us O lord, for these thy gifts, which we are about to receive, from thy bounty, through Christ our Lord, amen" and before the last vowel had a chance to dissipate, it was replaced with the sight and sounds of slashing forks hurriedly spearing food. If one was distracted and not paying close attention, the occasional howl of pain could be heard above the din of the feeding pack. "Pops, this meal is really good, you're going to make someone a nice wife someday", I said laughing. "Don't forget, your turn to do the dishes tonight, Bob", he said with a grin, "touché, dad touché".

After the last dish was washed, dried and placed into the cupboard, I was beginning to ponder what possible adventure this warm, starlit summer night might conjure up. "Hey dad, I am going to walk down to Dicks Drive In for cone", I shouted above the loud music emanating from the television, the unmistakable sounds of Hee Haw guaranteed that my dad would be glued to his well-worn Lazy Boy for the next hour. The screech of the back screen door announced my departure and as I walked towards my confectionary desire of a creamy vanilla ice cream encased in a hardened shell of sweet cherry dip. Walking slowly, I pulled the Winston from my shirt pocket and savored the first drag as I feed the nicotine beast.

Approaching the parking lot of Dicks Drive In, a car pulled into the lot and rolled to a stop. I watched, curiously, as the driver's window slowly rolled down. Within seconds, a familiar face emerged. "Hey bob, you got a minute" the familiar face inquired. "sure" I said, "what's up". That familiar face was a friend of my sister's boyfriend. With a toothy grin he proclaimed, "I am heading out to the lake and wanted to know if you would be interested in joining me", as he waited for my response, I pondered the offer. He was older than I, skinny and short, if it came to a fight, I knew I had him in the bag. So, I thought what the hell, a ride to the lake on this hot summer night sounded down right refreshing. As I slide into the passenger seat, he informed me that a small but necessary detour would be required. Nodding in approval, I rolled down the window, lit up a cigarette and enjoyed the sights and sounds of my home town as we headed towards his destination.

Turning off the smooth pavement of the main road, the sudden crunch of gravel being compressed communicated our arrival. He pulled up to the corner of the porch, its peeling paint indicated its age. As he turned off the ignition, the engine shuttered a few times and then stopped. Turning towards me he explained that he was picking up his date for the evening, "sure", I said. I watched, indifferent, as he bounded up the porch steps and then stopped at the front door. Reaching into his back pocket, he retrieved a comb and began to meticulously straighten his hair. "Come on man, ring the damn door- bell", I said to myself. "The night aint getting any younger", I muttered to myself. Placing the greasy comb back into his back pocket, he suddenly turned towards me and grinned, "come on, ring the door- bell" I shouted out. "Hey man, don't rush me", was his reply. With a sudden flick of his finger, I heard the audible sound of bells announcing the arrival of a guest and as the front door opened, out walked a cute girl, dark haired, dressed in cut-off jeans and a sleeveless pink button-down shirt, flashing the most beautiful smile. I had to admit I was taken a back, especially since my friend wasn't the most handsome kid in town. He politely escorted her to the vehicle, informed me to move to the back seat and then opened the front passenger door and politely helped her in. He strolled around the vehicle, and before he entered the car, he smiled and gave me that can't' believe it kind of wink. In a typical fourteen-year-old fashion, I rolled my eyes and gave him the middle finger salute

The red glow of my cigarette dimly illuminated the back seat, their awkward attempt at conversation was beginning to greatly annoy me and I was starting to strongly feel like the odd man out in this situation. Looking up I noticed that we had already passed the edge of town and were headed for to that algae bloom we call Lake Winnebago. With about five miles left to travel, he suddenly slowed and turned off the main highway onto a dark county road.

Looking up, I asked what was the problem, he looked at me in the rear-view mirror, for a few seconds and then turned around in the driver's seat and said the most incredible words to me, "Bob will you drive the car for me". Now I have had some experience driving the farm tractor around the fields and I have racked up some hours on the family's mini bike, but up to this moment, I have never driven a car on an actual road. Ummm, I pondered the question quite seriously for about three seconds then with a smile spread wide across my face and I could hear myself say, "SURE".

So, we exchanged our seating arrangements, I was now sitting in the driver's seat awkwardly gawking at the bright shiny gauges that were spread across the dashboard while he and his girlfriend were now in the back. I can remember that car, it was a 1960ish rambler with a push button transmission. I asked a few questions concerning what buttons I need to push to get this baby into drive while feeling around for the gas and brake pedals. After a few minutes of getting the feel, I pushed the drive button, applied a small amount of pressure on the gas pedal and viola, we were going down the road.

At first, my entire attention was spent on my driving, getting the feel of the steering, frequently checking my speed and relishing that feeling of pure driving joy, especially when you are engaged in an activity that is not quite lawful. I don't know how long my attention was focused purely upon myself but I suddenly became aware of some strange sounds coming from the tattered back seat of the car.

The unusual but frequent moans and groans at first startled me and I asked if everything was okay, he just told me reassuringly that everything was fine and I needed to just keep driving down the road. I wasn't too far down the road when those strange sounds started to repeat themselves.

Now my curiosity meter was starting to peg into the what the hell is that mode and to satisfy that curiosity, I reached up and moved the rearview mirror into a position that allowed me to view the activities in the back seat of that Rambler.

It was dark and I saw only glimpses of bare body parts engulfed in shadows and the harder I tried to see what was going on, the less attention I was paying to my driving. I began to stare into that little rectangular piece of glass with even more intensity, when all of sudden, did I see what I thought I saw, oh my god is that an actual woman's bare BREAST. As that thought was still echoing across my now hormone heightened brain, is when I heard the unmistakable sound of gravel being crushed by a two-thousand-pound automobile.

Jerking my eyes away from the rearview mirror and toward the roadway, I quickly realized with horror, that we were about to careen off the road and into the gaping mouth of a ditch. In a panic, I jerked hard on the steering wheel which then put the car half into the ditch and the other half of the car on the shoulder of the road, I could hear the grating sound of the under carriage as it ground away at the soil, my back seat passengers had now been flung to the floor board and the sounds of her screaming and his curses filled my ears.

My next maneuver was to pull the steering wheel back toward the road but I aggressively over corrected and the car swerved sharply out of the ditch, across the road and into the ditch on the other side. Looking into the rearview mirror, it looked like my passengers were hovering, defying the effects of gravity and then in the blink of an eye, they were thrown together onto the floor of the car. The screaming and cursing resumed.

For some unexplainable reason, I had forgot that the car had a mechanical device called brakes, my foot was still firmly planted upon the gas pedal and I was desperately trying to steer my way out of this situation. When suddenly, the yellow glow of the headlights was now illuminating the appearance of a sharp bend in the roadway.

With the car still running parallel to the road, half in the ditch, half on the road, I turned the front tires hard towards the road. The car was now grinding and throwing dirt as it followed the contour of the corner but the friction was now causing the car to slow and with a final screeching shudder the car came to a halt.

For a brief moment, it was absolutely quiet, only the sound of our rapid breathing could be heard and then in a flash, they both started hollering and cursing at me as my friend was now attempting to crawl from the back seat into the front, apparently to beat me to a pulp. I opened the car door and dashed off across the fields towards the distant lights of my home town. As I lay in bed that night, I was so thankful that none of us were seriously hurt or worse, killed.

As I slowly drifted off to sleep images of the night played across the crevices of my mind, when all of a sudden, hey is that a woman's bare.

• • • •• • • • •• ••• •

The golden glow of the autumn sun, slung low upon the horizon, was casting a soft palette of delightful hues upon the homes and landscapes of my neighborhood. The cooling air felt refreshing, a respite from the summer heat. Down the street, the raucous sounds of Dick's Drive In filled the air with the sound of cars and motorcycles revving their engines, mingled with the laughter of gathered friends. As I approached this hometown landmark, the tantalizing smells of hamburgers and French fries punctuated the night air. Turning the corner of 18th street, I flipped up the collar of my high school letter jacket, as a shield against the chilly fall air and proceeded towards my rendezvous.

I have always enjoyed the walks through my home-town, it is a comforting feeling as you pass by the monuments of your life. Recalling childhood activities, challenging the monkey bars, chasing each other on the playground while the girls practiced jumping rope.

Making the right hand turn past the old Kaukauna Club Cheese factory, the lights of Kaukauna suddenly blazed bright. The old familiar buildings stood as sentinels each one greeting your passage. Reaching the bottom of the hill, I turned right onto Dodge Street and made the last push to my destination, a very familiar domicile on Hillcrest Drive.

Walking up the weathered driveway, I faintly heard loud conversations. I always felt, at that moment, just prior to entering into the residence, an excitement that raced through me. In the summer, that house had quite a reputation, it was the gathering place, a rendezvous for teenage kids looking for a good time.

Opening the front door, I was greeted by a chorus of cheers as the quests acknowledged my arrival. Making my way towards the refreshments, I greeted each guest as I went. Suddenly an overwhelming feeling that this was going to be another one for the books placed a huge grin upon my face.

Upon entering the kitchen, I saw Ray and Cud engaged in a lively conversation. The kitchen was our war room, the place where we laid out our plans. Grabbing a slice of store-bought pizza, I pulled up a chair and listened.

Cud was a gentle giant that was graced with a rather large abundance of natural strength. I have often wondered if he had ever engaged in sports either wrestling or football, there was no doubt he would have dominated. He had a fun-loving character but he also didn't suffer fools and woe to the soul who was about to get a taste of that Samson strength. There were two things that I definitely knew about Cud, he loved having a good time and he loved fast cars.

Popping the top off a fresh beer, I noticed Ray looking at me and after clearing his throat he says, "hey there's a party tonight", I looked at him foolishly and said "Yea, we are standing in the kitchen of one said party". He flashes me his toothy grin, leans close and says, "tonight, a bigger party, the kind of party that has an abundance of friends and fine-looking girls". "And where is this said party", I asked. Smiling he answers, "Terry Devalk's farm".

A sweet smile spread across my face, beer parties are great fun, but beer parties in the country that comes with a barn and no close nosey neighbors, are awesome.

The smell of cigarette smoke and cologne greeted me as we got into Cuds car. Turning the ignition key, the big eight cylinder growled to life. As he backed out of the driveway and turned onto the street, you knew this wasn't grandma's pooch.

Rolling down the road, he quickly shifted through the first few gears after we flew down Hillcrest Drive, we turned onto Dodge Street and then finally onto Hwy 55. As we cruised out of town, I leaned into the back seat and listened to the music that now drifted out of the car's massive speakers,

As I daydreamed about what experiences this party was about to offer, I noticed we had turned onto county road CE. The road to Terry's place was just a few miles ahead. It was at that moment I felt the car quickly pick up speed, my heart raced as the needle on the speedometer buried itself, a crash at this velocity would vaporize your remains. In the dimly lit interior of the car, I saw that familiar smile spread across Cud's face, looking into the rearview mirror he screamed, POWERSLIDE.

As the car roared down CE and as the turn off to Terrys was fast approaching, Cud suddenly placed the car into a slide, I mean we were sliding down CE at over a hundred miles an hour, completely sideways. The sound of screeching tires filled the cabin as the smell of burnt rubber became overwhelming. Time seemed to stop and without a doubt I could feel my ass puckering tighter than a snare drum while my heart was attempting to leave my chest. At that moment, I really thought I was about to earn my angel wings, but to my surprise he clutched, slapped down a gear and hit the gas. The car shuttered as a few laws of physics kicked in and then amazingly we made a perfect transition onto Terry's Road.

For a brief moment all was silent and then the loudest whoops and hollers permeated the car's interior. We were all greatly relieved that the power slide was executed flawlessly and we hadn't suddenly become the towns next funeral procession. To be honest, after that adrenaline driven event, I don't remember much about the party, But I am sure I had a great time, but the memory of that heart throbbing, death defying feat will live on to eternity.

• •• • • •• ••• • •••

The thick cotton towel felt good against my skin, as my mom dried me off after my turn in the old porcelain bath tube. She quickly dressed me in my soft Roy Rodgers pajamas and a pair of slippers shaped as black cowboy boots complete with white spurs, and lastly, I belted on the shiny twin cap guns to finish off the attire. After I had finished dressing, I was off to catch a ride on my rocking horse, a blonde beauty called Trigger. I had about twenty-five minutes to complete a well imagined western scene, complete with rustling up villainous outlaws and saving the day for the towns law abiding citizens, because as soon as my younger sister was bathed, dried and dressed it was time to go.

As I slid into the back seat of my dads' car, I could hardly contain my excitement, one or two Saturdays a month, during the summer, our dad would take my sisters Gail, Debbie and myself to one of our favorite places, Dicks Drive In. I would roll the window down and let the balmy summer air wash over my face as the sounds of summer entertained my ears. For a boy of seven the drive from our house located on 7th Street and Kenneth Avenue to Dicks Drive seemed to take forever. And how we would sit upright, straining to see that neon sign that signaled we were close. Closing one's eyes, images of cold ice cream topped with all of its' possible confections danced merrily in a young child's mind.

As we turned onto the parking lot, the bright neon lights greeted us, the rule was ,we were allowed one of anything on the menu, O my, was it going to be a vanilla cone or a chocolate cone, let's not forget the vanilla chocolate swirl or the vanilla cone dipped in a variety of toppings such as cherry or butterscotch, maybe tonight it would be the root beer float or the chocolate sundae, at times it was simply mind boggling. But in most instances after I had carefully weighed my options, I would order the banana split. I loved that combinations of flavors that so tantalized my taste buds, two slices of banana topped with vanilla ice cream, topped with chocolate, topped with caramel, topped with whip cream, topped with cherries and finally topped with nuts. All contained in a plastic boat served up with a plastic spoon. By the end of the summer, I had a flotilla of plastic boats floating through the suds of my bubble bath while my baking soda submarine, just ten box tops and twenty-five cents, was sending those plastic battleships down to Davey Jones locker.

The summer of my ninth year was now drawing to a close, I had no clue just how much Dicks Drive In was about to become an integral part

[103]

of my life. January twenty eighth 1965, my tenth birthday, dawned bright but bitterly cold. The red colored mercury on the thermometer, outside of our frosted kitchen window, was dipped below the zero number and hovered somewhere near the, damn that's cold, minus six-degree mark. I actually looked that temperature up on wunderground.com, wow the internet. Now, I was sitting at the kitchen table feeling rather depressed while a flurry of activity from my parent's friends were energetically whisking boxes and furniture out of our house into the frigid outdoors and then into a fleet of cars and trucks.

We were moving, I had no idea where, and instead of the abnormal attention one receives on their birthday, I was instead left unattended and seemly forgotten. As the last items of our house were loaded, I climbed into our car and watched the only house I had ever known, and my best friends' house, slowly disappear through the oval rear window of my dads' car. At this moment in my life, I never felt lonelier.

Tears clouded my eyes as we drove to our shiny new residence, I didn't even watch our progress, my head was hung down, my hands clasped together, I couldn't believe this was happening on my birthday. The car finally came to a stop and my dad exclaimed, "here we are", I looked up and had my first glimpse of our new house. It had plank siding, painted a yellowish, gold, instead of the shingle siding our old house had. The cape cod house stood sturdy upon its masonry block foundation and the double car garage didn't lean precariously as our previous garage did, *"I bet this garage doesn't even have any bats hanging upside down",* I thought grumpily. Sitting at the kitchen table I felt sorry for myself as Rita and Jean Verhagen and others happily helped my parents in unloading their precious cargo.

Suddenly, my mom stopped and leaned down and planted a kiss on my forehead, "What's the matter honey", she said, just then another burst of tears gushed forth, "You forgot my birthday", I blurted out. "Ah I'm sorry sweetie that we had to move today, but forget your birthday I think not". Then my dad appeared carrying a birthday cake, with ten candles blazing while my parents and their friends belted out a chorus of Happy Birthday. My frown abruptly turned into a smile and as all of those friendly faces were wishing me a happy birthday someone whispered into my ear, "and Dicks Drive In is just four doors down", this, I thought, just might not be so bad after all.

The hot sticky summer night felt oppressive as we chased each other around our neighborhood playing a game called the Fox and the Hounds. Some unfortunate soul is picked the hound and the rest are foxes, the object of the game is for the hound to literally tag a fox which turns that person into a hound and on and on until there is one fox left, which when tagged is declared the winner.

As the sweat dripped down my face and onto the soft summer grass, my ears suddenly picked up the distant sound of shoes rapidly slapping the ground. And that sound appeared to be heading straight for my hidden position. When the tagged hound was mere feet from my hiding space I bolted out of the shrubs and sprinted around the side of the house and headed for the opposite side of the street. As I ran, the rapid breathing of the hound seemed to be gaining on me, damn I thought it must be Norman, a short individual that possessed the speed of a jack rabbit.

While making a hard right turn around Reinholtz's house I tripped on some invisible obstacle and with a loud groan and a thud, I impacted mother earth. Within seconds, I heard that accursed phrase, "tag your now a hound buddy". I laid upon the ground for a few minutes to catch my breath and while slowly climbing to my feet I heard someone nearby call out the time. In a heartbeat, we were all running for that delightful destination, Dicks Drive In.

Every night in the summer, Mister Sternhagen would pick two of us to clean up the parking lot and the area around the picnic tables and our reward for said work was the ability to freely pick one item from the menu. As we huddled around the order window, Mister Sternhagen would stick his head out the window and with a grin, he would point out the two lucky youngsters. While the two lottery winners went quickly about their business, the others would groan and then quietly wait for the winners, Mister. Sternhagen always made sure that everyone got an equal chance to earn those drive in delights.

The winters cold grip was slowly losing its influence; the remaining piles of snow were now turning into wet slushy substances that left one's feet wet and cold. Norman and I were walking home and as we walked past Dicks Drive In, he suddenly stopped and attempted to open the side door. Dicks Drive In was closed through the cold and blustery winter and re-opened when the snows had melted and the robins had made their return. That previous summer, he had constructed a new windowed enclosure around the front of the order window to provide protection from the elements. And to our surprise the side door was open even though the drive in was weeks away from turning out its culinary treats.

Laughing we sauntered up to the order window and made ridiculous orders, "I'll take a thousand hamburgers and two thousand fries" "and

[105]

don't forget the cheese on them their burgers", we laughed ourselves silly, but unbeknownst to us, some citizen had witnessed two eleven-year-olds enter the drive in that was not yet open. As we walked across the parking lot a police car pulled up and two officers got out and questioned us about entering Dicks Drive In, I don't know if Norman was protecting me but he answered first and explained he was the only one that had entered Dicks Drive In, I was shocked as the officers placed Norman in the back of the car and left. I went running home, terrified that I was next.

The next day Norman came over and explained that the police had taken him downtown and called Mister Sternhagen and Norman's parents. It was quite apparent that we were not the hardened criminals the concerned citizen thought we were and he was left to the custody of his parents. For years after, I swung a wide berth around those side doors when Dicks Drive In was closed.

I opened the back door of my dads' house and before even I got to the kitchen, I heard my mom call out. "Bob Charlie ran away again". With a sad shake of my head and a purposefully loud groan I replied, "Can't Mary go and look for Charlie this time". "She already did and she couldn't find hair nor tail of him", she replied back. I sat down grumpily upon the hard kitchen chair and became rather upset with my current assignment, my feet hurt and I was tired after working on the farm all day, besides the smell of manure clinging to my clothes was a sure give away to Charlie that I was on the approach. With a loud sigh I pushed myself up from the comfort of the kitchen chair and headed for the back door, "damn you Charlie" I muttered under my breath.

The screen door screeched and shuttered as I left the house, now the question was, where to start. Charlie was our newest house resident, a beagle that loved to eat, sleep and hump any unsuspecting individual's leg or some unfortunate pillow. He also loved to escape the house and the boundaries of our property, and if he had the chance, as soon as a door opened and he was within sprint distance, zoom past you he ran, out the door and he kept on running no matter how much yelling you inflicted upon him. It wasn't until later that we found his kryptonite, accidently one day, as he was dashing for freedom across our backyard my mother uttered a series of cuss words that made me blush, we discovered if you screamed at the top of your lungs, every curse word that belonged to mankind, he would slam on the brakes and walk back home, tail between his legs. Man, who knew.

As I walked up the street, begrudgingly, calling his name and looking for any sight of that wayward hound, I kept telling myself, if I was Charlie where would I be hanging out. Maybe the people on seventeenth street have a new dog, or maybe Charlie is attempting to make a new friend or a lover if the gender was right.

After that lead fizzled out, I headed across the empty lot between Seventeenth Street and Eighteenth Streets that brought me to the back of Dicks Drive In and there exhausted I parked myself on one of the picnic tables to take a break. As I looked up, I couldn't believe my eyes, there standing next to one of the side doors was Charlie. I was astounded; I couldn't believe my sudden good fortune.

As I pushed my dirty, tired body up from the picnic table, to retrieve our family pet, I stopped and stared in amazement. A customer walked up to the side door and on cue, Charlie began his performance, standing on his hind legs and offering his front paw for a shake, and if that didn't get his desired response, he would roll over or play dead. The customer would laugh and then in disbelieve, as the customer exited the drive In, they produced for Charlie a hamburger or a hot dog. I sat back down upon the green, wooden seat of the picnic table and watched the one dog circus display.

After I crushed out my second cigarette, I stood up and proceeded in the direction of Charlie. Upon reaching our family canine, he looked up and if a dog could smile, I swear he was grinning from ear to ear. I looked down into his big brown eyes and said rather calmly, "come on Charlie it's time to go home". And to my surprise he lifted himself up and started walking, without encouragement, towards home.

As I followed behind that long eared, short legged pooch, I started to giggle and then that giggle turned into a laugh so vigorous that in no time my ribs ached. His playful performance was so successful that his belly was actually dragging on the ground from consuming so much of Dicks Drive In's culinary treats. "Be careful Charlie" I giggled to myself, "to much drive in food could clog up those arteries."

The early fall maple leaves had started its yearly transition from chlorophyll green to brilliant reds and oranges. I was lying in bed blowing blueish white smoke rings that chased each other up, spread out and then disappeared upon impact with the ceiling. It rattled me a little when I heard a knock on my bedroom window. Raising up upon my bed and, with a bewildered look, I gazed out the window to discover the source of that sound. There standing on her tiptoes with her golden hair flowing down past her shoulders was a very good friend of mine, Wendy

Miller. I opened the window and inquired as to why she was knocking on my window instead of the door. I saw she was crying and I softly replied that I would be right out. As I sat on the edge of my bed putting on my shoes I was starting to ponder as to what could be upsetting her so. Maybe an argument with parents or her boyfriend. I walked down the back hall and opened the screen door and there she was sitting, presenting such a forlorn figure. "Hey girl what's up", was my standard statement for such occasions. She looked up at me and said "can we walk and talk for a while", "sure" I said. We walked side by side for a while not speaking a word.

Finally, we got to Dicks Drive In and plunked ourselves down on one of his green painted picnic tables. She dug around in her unorganized purse and pulled out a pack of Kool's and then proceeded to look for her lighter. I reached into my stained shirt pocket and pulled out my Bic and offered her a light. After taking a few deep drags she looked me in the eye and said those words that I wasn't even remotely prepared for. She had cancer and she was going to be gone for a period of time at the Mayo Clinic receiving treatment. I was stunned, usually a person of many words, I couldn't think of anything to say. We sat quietly for a while, smoking cigarettes and listening to the carefree laughter and music that surrounded Dicks Drive In. She leaned her head on my shoulder and at that moment the dam broke and tears began to stream down my face. I do believe that there are some events that words cannot convey any form of comfort, only the squeezing of a hand or the lending of a shoulder seems to be more adequate. We listened and watched the healthy human activity until Dicks Drive In's bright neon lights shuttered to darkness and in the silence, I walked her home.

That summer before our senior year, we young males were feeling our oats. Just one more year and we would be able to enter, fully, into the adult world. I remember hanging out with my friends as we strutted ourselves for the benefit of the young fillies hanging out at Dicks Drive In, when we heard the awful news. One of our friend's, Mark Rennicke, had been shot. In a few hours, as the news spread, kids gathered in the parking lot of the Kaukauna Hospital. We stood around, stunned, attempting to console each other, yearning to hear some good news. His dad informs us, that he was experiencing brain swelling and the doctors were attempting to reduce it. We sat for hours; I don't even know what time in the early morning we got the news that Mark didn't make it. I remember weeping so hard that I couldn't continue to drive, I pulled into the back of Dicks Drive In and cried for some time. I couldn't understand how someone so young and vital could be taken away so suddenly. It shattered my adolescent sense of invincibility; he was my first friend that I lost and it affected me for years after.

The actual graduation seemed to take forever, and having the last name of Zierler, I was the last one to stand upon the stage and receive my official notice that I had graduated High School. For twelve years my life was pretty routine, survive nine months of school and then enjoy summer vacations.

Now I had entered into the full-time work force and my father's rules were fairly rigid, you could stay at home and go to a local higher learning institute and pay rent or get a full-time job and get to living on your own. I decided upon the full-time job experience. Excitedly, I placed the last few worn boxes of my remaining possessions into the back of my car, walked back into the house and offered my good byes.

As I stood by the door of my new car a 1973 Plymouth Cuda, a gift to myself for entering the adult world, I lit up a Pall Mall and stood there gazing out upon my neighborhood. So many great and sad things had happened since I moved here on my tenth birthday, mostly great things and for that I was deeply grateful. I couldn't help but feel a sense of sadness leaving this small patch of earth that I had called home. But it was time to move on, to allow the next generation of youngsters to dominate that neighborhood. I backed the car out of the driveway and headed for my new residence.

As I drove past Dicks Drive In, I couldn't help but realize how much that business had become a part of my life. After unpacking my last few belongings into my new apartment, I heard a knock on the door, after peering through the key hole and I was surprised to see a close friend of mine named Paul. He looked me in the eye and said "are you hungry", "sure I said, let me get my wallet".

As we got into his car I said "Dicks Drive In", he said "why drive there, just a few blocks away is an A&W," I smiled and thought, I do believe this is going to work out just fine.

• • • •• • • • • •• •

Thirty, an innocuous number, nothing special, not even a prime number, easily divisible, its claim to fame is it belongs to eleven of the twelve months and it was the number of silver coins paid for Judas's betrayal. Um, but that number has a much more significant meaning for me, so let me lift the impairing fog of days past and present my case against that seemly innocent figure, the number 30.

This particular fall was spectacular, the brilliant golds, reds and oranges of fall leaves, bereft of chlorophyll, painted the landscape and the cool mornings and comfortable afternoons were a great respite from the hot and humid ravages of summer. This time of the year held two very special activities for me, chasing the wily and highly prized whitetail deer and the ability to play a gladiator style contest that involved an inflated pigskin and an arena called the gridiron.

I awoke much earlier than usual and as soon as my head left the pillow, the butterflies began their annoying game within me. "Damn, I don't understand why after four years of football, I still get such strong pre-game jitters", I muttered to myself. As my feet touched the floor, the cold of the linoleum on my bare feet, which usually felt soothing during the warm mornings of summer, now felt rather annoying on this cool fall day.

I walked into the kitchen and cracked open the refrigerator and groped around for the gallon of whole milk, upon retrieval of a bowl and spoon, I next searched for my favorite source of breakfast energy, nope not Wheaties, for me it was Captain Crunch.

As the cold, white milk sporadically flowed over the edges of my overfilled cereal bowl, I began my usual ritual of reading the mornings newspaper, for some reason only three sections of the paper ever held my interest, the sports page, the funnies and the orbits. As the loud crunching of the captain filled my ears, my sister appeared, wearing her well-worn but comfortable bathrobe, "morning Bob", she said, "are you ready for the big game", she continued, "hell sis I was born ready", I replied as milk dripped from my mouth and dribbled down my chin. "Damn Bob, were you born in the basement and never brought up, don't talk with your mouth full" she lamented, "Okay sis", I replied, as another portion of milk slithered down my chin. "Disgusting, just disgusting", she muttered.

After draining the last delicious ounce of Captain Crunch flavored milk, I quickly made my way to the only upstairs bathroom of the house, with three sisters, it was important to obtain that first bathroom position. Closing the bathroom door, I heard my sisters insistent muttering, "How long are you going to take Bob, you know I have to do my hair", the rest just sounded like blah, blah, blah.

The walk to school was feeling rather brisk but the warmth of my letter jacket helped in keeping the frigid temperatures at bay. As I passed through the empty lot adjacent to Dicks Drive In, I helped myself to one of the ripened, red apples hanging deliciously from one of the branches. This was not just another game against one of our rivals, this was our ritual homecoming game where the joyful atmosphere of the dance hinged upon our ability to provide our school a victory.

Upon entering the front doors of my high school, I quickly proceeded to my home room for early morning roll call. As I headed to my first morning class the sound of my hard soled shoes echoed loudly down the hall. I suddenly realized more students than usual was smiling and acknowledging my presence. "Shit", I muttered to myself, "thanks but I really don't need the added pressure".

During the last class of the day, for some reason, the clocks in the school ran at a much slower pace than during any other school period. Seconds seemed like minutes and minutes seemed like hours. The anticipation of Saturday's game was growing more intense as the day progressed and when the final bell rang, I could barely contain my excitement.

That evening was the traditional parade and the ritual painting of an old donated car in the school colors of our opponents, and then as the crowd roared and cheered, students took turns with a sledge hammer, battering that opposing symbol. As the colorful parade and its arousing activities began to die down, I turned the collar of my leather jacket up and made the long, lonely and cold walk home.

Saturday morning broke sunny and clear and the butterflies inside had turned it up a notch or two, at least the nausea I felt wasn't strong enough for me to skip breakfast. I was thankful that I had, regrettably, turned down the many party offers which meant besides the pregame anxiety, I didn't also have to deal with a hangover. As I donned my blue jeans and my faded T-shirt, I started to run down the checklist for the day's activities, clean the car, check, have the suit dry cleaned, check, make the dinner reservations, check, and retrieve from my dresser drawer the thirty dollars for the homecoming dinner, check. I had to work extra hours at the Piggly Wiggly grocery store to save the extra thirty dollars required and I was guarding that hard earned money as if it was a gold-filled payroll box.

The car sputtered a few times and then roared to life, "I've got to get that choke fixed" I reminded myself as I sat quietly in the driver's seat. A few minutes had passed as I dialed up a radio station, allowing the V8 to warm up. The static buzz of the white noise was becoming quite annoying when suddenly the sound of Creedence Clear Water Revival filled the spaces of my cream colored, Ford Galaxy. Placing the transmission into reverse, I backed out the driveway and headed towards the game's destiny.

The ammonia smell of sweat infused practice jerseys and unwashed socks along with the aroma of icy hot hung heavy in the locker room air. I always arrived a little early, it allowed me to settle into my game face and to go over the new plays designed specifically for our opponent. Besides, the comradery of my fellow teammates helped with the anxiety and nervousness that came with being an athlete.

I had partially suited up and was sitting on the medical table cutting it up with Pat while he expertly applied the sticky, white, sports tape to my ankles, when suddenly the sound of music filled the locker room., yep, Bob Peebles had arrived. He was notorious for changing certain words in songs to bring out their true comedic meaning. And it wasn't long before the room was filled with strong male voices all singing Bob's new rendition of Venus by Shocking Blue, where he had replaced the word Venus with the word penis, to this day, I laugh so hard whenever I sing that song in his comedic style.

After talking with Ray, I laid down upon the wooden bench and tried to slow down my rapidly beating heart, I closed my eyes and imagined how I would play that day, as a defensive end, I needed to slightly hesitate before reaching the line of scrimmage to allow the gap in the line to naturally appear and then to make sure I turn any running play on my side to the inside. At last, the word went around, it was time to head to the field, As I raised myself up from the bench, I looked at Ray and smiled, "Ray this is going to be some kind of fun", he said, "let's go get em", as we all filed out and proceeded to the grass covered field, where teams of padded covered gladiators were about to engage in football combat.

While we were performing our pre-game warmups, we would routinely begin scouting out the other team. The first attribute we scouted for was size, the bigger a player meant the more intense the game, if they were physically smaller meant we hoped we had enough stretchers for their injured.

Last year and so far, this year, we had maintained being the number one defense in the Fox Valley League and we weren't about to give up that designation so easily. The opposing team was our familiar nemesis, Kimberly and judging by their physical size, it was going to be a hell of a game. As we lined up for the game opening kickoff, my adrenaline was kicked into muscle shaking, eye bulging, high gear. I watched Randy's kick soar high into the air as we sped down the field, I dodged the first would be blocker and shoulder brushed the second blocker. The spine jolting impact of the tackle drove me and the returner hard into the grass of the field, as I reached down to help him up, the pre-game butterflies were instantly gone, replaced by an intense desire to play and to play hard.

The game was a low score affair our defense was pretty stingy in not allowing scores while our offense worked hard for every point Kimberly would grudgingly give up, it was a close contest, somewhere in the second quarter, they were attempting a pitch out run to my side of the field, I ran past the first blocker and stuck out my right arm to ward off the second blocker. As we made contact, I felt a sharp sting in my right thumb, instead of keeping my hand flat, I had thrust it out in a choke hold position and his helmet slammed into the webbing between my thumb and my index finger. The pain was intense as I ran off the field clutching my right hand. The assistant coach took me off to the side and asked me what was wrong, "I think I dislocated my thumb", I painfully said, "here let me look at it", he said, grabbing my thumb and he gave it a hard pull. The sudden severe, sharp tingling pain shot from my hand up to my shoulder. I grimaced and lowered my head, "can you play" the coach asked, "sure, sure coach I can still play".

As soon as the current play was over, he sent me back into the game. As I attempted to get into my three-point stance, I noticed I couldn't touch my right hand on the ground, doing so sent sharp tingling pain up my right arm. I tried my best to continue my pre-injury performance but any contact to that injured thumb resulted in searing pain, so I started trying to tackle with one arm, which was painful and not very effective. Kimberly began to capitalize on the situation and started running more plays in my direction and they were now gaining more yards per play.

At half-time, I sat alone dejected as Pat tried to tape my right thumb to help in minimizing the now constant ache and throbbing. Our head coach came over and read me the riot act about not helping in shutting down my side of the defense. I could only shake my head in painful agreement, "I'll do better in the second half coach", I stammered, I was at the verge of telling him about the frightful pain in my right thumb, but as with most athlete's, my pride prevented that conversation.

As the third quarter progressed, I gritted my teeth and played through the pain, the constant contact had converted the sharp, stinging pain to more of a numbness and my play improved. As we lined up, I felt Ray tap my right buttocks, which meant, I was to charge to the outside while he stunted to the inside. At the snap of the ball, I shot past the tight end and was free and clear in the backfield, they were, once again, attempting a quick pitch to my side and because of my position in the backfield, I was quickly bearing down on the running back for what was to be a three-or four-yard loss.

Just as I was lowering my shoulder for the tackle, I heard a sharp crack and then I was falling to the ground, bewildered as to what had happened, there was nobody in front or to the side of me, so I rolled over and attempted to stand up, I couldn't get my feet under me so I rolled over on my back and lifted my now painful left leg into the air, at first it didn't register, I could see my leg, but instead of a foot pointing skyward at the end, there was a blunt stump, I lifted my leg even higher and then I saw that my foot was completely dislocated, with both broken leg bones pushing hard against the skin, my foot was now hanging against the back of my calf with the toes pointing in the wrong direction. The first scream actually sounded inside of my head, I remember that, but the second scream escaped my lips and rang loudly in my ears, without lowering my leg, I lowered my head against the now intense pain and pressure I was beginning to feel.

I remember Ray holding my hand as the game Doctor grabbed my foot and with a violent pull and twist, set my foot back in place, I could feel the muscles tear and the bones grate as they shifted back into their normal anatomical position, but, thank God, at least the intense pain and pressure was gratefully relieved. I felt tremendous disappointment that I couldn't finish the game with my fellow teammates, almost as if I was purposely letting them down.

As soon as the stretcher was placed on the sidelines, the ambulance crew began placing a plastic cast upon the injured limb, once in place, they pumped up the cast with air to stabilize the injury and then off to the ER I went.

As I lay upon the emergency room table, a staff of nurses were removing and cutting off my uniform while the radiologists were taking x-rays of my leg. I remember asking them if they could bring in a radio so I could listen to the end of the game.

After they had left, my family physician Doctor Simon Cherkasky entered the room and began his examination, he moved my foot back and forth and as he did so I could feel and hear the bones clicking against their broken ends, "can you hear that", he said, "hear it doc, I can feel it and the next time you do that, I swear I'll break your nose", I hollered back. He smiled, "sorry", he said, "I have looked at the x-rays and I have consulted with an orthopedic surgeon, you are going to require plates and bolts to repair that lower leg injury", he exclaimed. "Okay doc" I said, "by the way can you look at my thumb", I said, now swollen and discolored. He examined it and said, "let's take an x-ray" and out the ER door he went as the radiology team re-entered the room.

As I laid upon the hard cold examination table, listening to the game, Doctor Cherkasky came back into the room with the x-ray of my hand, he placed that x-ray image in the viewer on the wall, switched on the bright light and exclaimed, "What the hell did you do to your hand", "I hurt it earlier in the game", I tried to explain, "goddamn it Bob, that thumb is broken clean away from the rest of your hand, we now also need to pin that back in place", he shouted at me. "Oh shit" was all I could muster to say. As they moved me from the ER to my room, the radio never left my side and my fellow teammates fought back and snatched the victory away from Kimberly for a Kaukauna win.

After the game, my teammates and coaches came by to offer their condolences and their words of encouragement. And as the sun set pink against the horizon, the emotional events of the day plus the fact that I wasn't going to be enjoying the homecoming dinner and dance began to weigh heavy upon me, and it wasn't long until the warm tears began to cascade down my face.

After I had awakened from the effects of the anesthesia, the surgeon was standing at the foot of my bed, "good news", he said, "we successfully repaired the injury with two stainless-steel plates and four bolts", "but the bad news is the complete dislocation of your ankle was pretty severe, there may be a chance you'll never be able to run again", he proclaimed. Still groggy from the surgery, I smiled and said, "we'll just have to see about that".

It took over one complete year for me to just be able to hobble down the track, the amount of bone re-growth was pretty expansive, my left ankle was better than twice the size of my right ankle and if I landed wrong on my left foot, the whole ankle would just lock up. I would grimace and cuss attempting to get it to revolve again. But persistence can be the true engine of change, I refused to give up and I started hobbling a mile, and then jogging a mile as I watched my left ankle begin to shrink. Within two years I was running again three miles, then five miles, then eight miles and then up to ten miles and I was back to boxing. At the age of twenty-eight, I joined the Army and blew through basic training, maintaining a twelve-to-thirteen-minute two mile runs throughout my eight years of service. After a twenty-five mile; Army hump in the desert, we were setting up our pup tents for the night, my right ankle was sore from the walk in the soft sands of the desert but my left ankle, which could only pronate about half as much as my normal right ankle, was as solid as a rock. I took off my boots and looked at the still larger left ankle and said, "we've come a long way buddy, thanks for your service".

I remember reviewing the game film, I hadn't seen the Kimberly player because he hit me from behind, a clip, a dirty play. What was ironic, the previous year, this same player had sprained his ankle towards the end of the game and I helped him off the field. Sad isn't it. He ended my football career but he didn't dampen my spirit. I went on to win the Wisconsin heavy weight boxing championship and had a fine military career, serving in Desert Storm.

Oh, by the way what does this story have to do with the number thirty you ask, what I am about to say is the gospel truth, I learned that on September 30th, I broke my right thumb at approximately 1:30, broke my left leg at approximately 2:30, I had 30 dollars stolen from my locker and yes if you remember my football number it was 30. But the great news is the jinx of that number was replaced by the blessing of that same number as I married the girl of my dreams, Christine Kamke, on June 30th in Bexar County Texas. It reminded me how great God truly is.

• • • •• • •••• •• • • • •

As I stood outside the faded and aging Veterans of Foreign Wars building, I reached into my jacket pocket and fished out a Winston cigarette, striking a match, I placed the sulfurous flame to the end of my cigarette and observed the opaque white smoke rise up and quietly watched as it was carried adrift upon the breeze. I always felt both excited and nervous as I stood upon the threshold of the Friday night dance. Taking in a breath I gathered myself and prepared to enter its portal.

The red sparks of the lit tobacco raced across the parking lot as I crushed out my cigarette, taking a deep breath to calm my nerves, I slowly began the ascent into the venue. As I paid my admission, I couldn't help but notice the glistening gleam of perspiration that accumulated upon my hands, a telltale sign of my anxious anticipation.

As I stared at the freshly introduced ink stamp, I heard a familiar voice, above the noise, call out my name. From out of the crowd, the smiling face of my friend Ray Kappell appeared. We stood upon the worn and scarred hardwood planks and screamed into each other's ears to be heard above the din and the loud music. As with most males of the day, we slowly sauntered over to an empty place by the wall and began our survey of the young and energetic crowd.

The usual visuals quickly registered, most of the males were standing, holding up the walls, while the young girls were dancing in friendly groups, swaying to the music and talking in excited tones. Scanning the dance floor, I suddenly spotted the girl that I had danced with last week, she was wearing a blue satin dress and her light brown hair bounced softly to the beat. Perspiration began to dampen my shirt and my heart quickened as I fought my fear to go out onto the dance floor.

My fearful trance was disrupted as Ray suddenly appeared and asked if I wanted to go outside for a quick smoke. Following his lead, we weaved our way through the throngs of kids and then left the building. The cool night air felt good against our perspiring skin as we took turns lighting our filtered cigarettes.

Looking around, I saw there were small groups of kids, standing in pockets around the building, some talking and laughing passionately, while others stood quietly and observed. Ray and I had just about finished smoking our cigarettes when another friend walked up, it was

[117]

Pat. Pat was a rather lovable and fun individual, you always knew whenever Pat was around, things could get very interesting.

He brought our attention to a group of boys that were wearing colorful rival letter jackets and mumbled some statement like, "I think I'll go over and say hi" and before I could clearly ascertain what he had said or what his intentions were, he left our side and to my utter amazement, walked over to that tightly encircled group of young men, crawled between one of their legs, stood up into their surprised midst and let loose a fairly good hay maker. In the ensuing chaos, he had run back to Ray and myself and as that group of boys discovered his whereabouts, they proceeded into our direction without due haste.

I looked at Ray, Ray looked at me, and before the fiery red sparks of my distinguishing cigarette had dissipated, they were upon us. The loud grunts and groans of bodies engaged in the fighting sports quickly drew a crowd of onlookers. Unfortunately for our rivals, Ray, Pat and I were fairly skilled in the art of combat sports and we had swiftly and decisively subdued our opponents. As I was brushing off the dirt and straightening my clothing, I could see Pat wearing his famous smile that expressed both elation and satisfaction.

Regaining our composure, we re-entered the dance as the heavy bass of a Black Sabbath song strongly vibrated through our bodies, as I, along with most of the other males, continued our slow circle around the dance floor, as if in a symbolic mating ritual as the young ladies swayed and writhed in a series of seductive dance gestures. I can remember the heavy tension and I always felt the duality of the situation, the desire to be dancing in rhythm, alongside a lovely lass, against the fear I had of making a complete ass out of myself. I started to look for that brown-haired beauty that I had seen earlier when a sudden loud disturbance caught my attention.

A group of seniors had burst angrily into the dance hall, that was usually reserved for freshmen and sophomores; they strode boldly through the crowd, with their gaze fixated upon one individual. In those days, we had a boy that was a type of Fonzi, except he was the dark side of Fonzi, always dressed in a black leather jacket, with his hair combed back into an oily duck style of the 50's, he prowled our ranks, bullying kids, his presence always dampened the atmosphere and added a sense of fear. He was older than us and his bulking size added to his mean demeanor. But this night, he had beat up the wrong boy for his older brother and his friends had arrived to extract their pound of flesh. The beating that he took was almost unbearable to witness, at one point I actually feared that they were going to kill him.

As the ruckus moved outside and the dance music resumed, I left the dance floor and headed downstairs to the refreshment stand. Waiting impatiently for my turn, I was suddenly pleasantly surprised to see the girl of my earlier fancy. She was sipping on a soda and quietly conversing with a close friend when our eyes made contact. In an instant I could see that look of recognition in her eyes and then a slow smile started to spread across her face. I swallowed hard a couple of times, gathered up my courage and walked over. "Hi" I said, "how are you". She looked up at me, then hesitated a few awkward moments, and finally said "fine", "I'm doing fine". We both looked sheepishly down at our feet, searching for something interesting to say, when she abruptly said, "I am about to go back upstairs, would you care to join me". Without saying a word, she slipped her hand into mine and led me back to the dance floor.

We danced and laughed as the sweat poured down our bodies, the first hours of trepidation had finally faded away, replaced with the pure joy of the dance. As the lights of the dance hall dimmed, we all knew it time for what most boys yearned for, the slow dance. As the Moody Blues slow beat reverberated through the hall, we danced in slow tight circles, our bodies sensuously touching, our heads laid upon each other's shoulders. I could smell the flowered scent of her shampoo along with the fragrance of her perfume, it was one of those moments you wished would never end, but suddenly the glare of the bright lights is turned back on and instantly, that magic moment begins to vanish.

I walked her home, hand in hand, exchanging smiles and light hearted conversations. As we stopped on her front porch, we talked for a bit, each one waiting quietly for the other to initiate the good night kiss. I stopped talking, took a long look into those soft brown eyes and then we kissed. I remember the walk home felt as if I was floating, recalling the dance and the kiss over and over again. As I turned up the driveway to my house, I looked up and said out loud, "thanks Vets for a lovely evening".

• • • •• • • •• • •

As I awoke, I was greeted by the musty smell of the couch cushions that I had decided to take a nap upon. The phonograph was playing the loud, raspy sound of a needle going around and around at the end of an album, Steppenwolf I believe. Rolling up into a sitting position, I rubbed the sleep from my eyes. My brain was frantically attempting the transition from a dream to reality. When a memory suddenly popped up, oh yah, tonight was the party at one of our favorite locations, a beautiful rustic farm located not far from the wonderful, green shores of Lake Winnebago. With a sense of renewed purpose, I shot up from the couch and raced up the basement stairs. "Hey Mom", I hollered, as I entered the kitchen, "are my favorite jeans clean". "Who do you think I am, the house maid", She replied, as I ran down the hall to my bedroom, Smiling, I hollered back, "Why of course you are, but you do know you're the prettiest house maid in the neighborhood".

After a long hot shower, I walked to the kitchen, decorated in yellow, where my dad promptly addressed me, "Bob, do I look like I'm made out of money, those thirty-minute showers are killing me". Pretending not to notice, I quickly got dressed, combed my hair and piled on a liberal amount of cheap cologne. As I headed out, my dad asked, "Where are you headed to son", without missing a beat, I shot back, "I'm heading to Louie Millers farm".

Strolling over to my 1963, cream colored two door Ford Galaxy, I pulled a fresh Winston from my shirt pocket, struck a match and lit it up. After opening the heavy car door, I gracefully slide into the worn and stained driver's seat.

As I turned the key; I heard the sound of the solenoid clicking as my starter refused to engage. I turned the key to the off position, threw out a few choice cuss words and then cranked it again. This time, the engine spun then with a sudden cough and shutter the powerful V8 engine roared to life.

I gently eased the car out of the driveway and backed out onto 18th street. After waiting somewhat impatiently at the corner of 18th street and Crooks Avenue, I finally turned left and headed out towards the freshly manured pastures of the countryside.

The analog music of the radio stations was fading in and out and occasionally interrupted by the static sounds of the speakers, which was painfully assaulting my ears. I was Searching for a rock station when out

[120]

of the blue, the magic sound of Stairway to Heaven suddenly filled the interior of my car. Rolling down the car window I felt the cool breeze flowing heavenly over me while the smell of fresh cut grass hung heavy in the air. It wasn't long before I turned onto highway 114, laying on the accelerator, I made the final push to Louie's farm.

The sound of driveway gravel popping and crunching under my tires meant I had arrived. As I pulled onto the farm. I saw a fair number of quests had already arrived, indicated by their cars parked helter-skelter across the farm's driveway and lawn. My heartrate quickened a bit, with anticipation, as I parked my car. The minute I stood up, I pulled the black comb from my back pocket and made sure my hair was perfect. As I opened the front door, the muffled sounds of an active party quickly gained in clarity and decibels.

Crossing over the threshold, I saw my friends enjoying both the atmosphere and the company. It wasn't long before someone had thrust an ice-cold beer into my hand and as the sound waves of the Beatles vibrated through my body, I found my friends, Louie, Rod and Bob. As the party spilled out around us, we talked about music since Bob was an accomplished guitar player and then the conversation turned to the science of self-defense.

At the time, I was an amateur boxer in the newly founded Kaukauna boxing club and I was fairly curious to discuss the differences in the self-defense arts since Bob and Rod were both taking Karate classes. After the four or five beers, that I had already consumed, began to strip away my common sense, I asked Bob to perform a side kick to my chiseled chest. I was entertaining the suggestion that my boxers' physique was strong enough to overcome such a blow.

Bob looked incredulous back at me and then asked me to repeat the request. Smiling he said something like "Are you sure", I gave him my confident go-ahead nod as I puffed out my chiseled chest. He set down his beer, smiled, and planted a side kick that firmly landed my backside onto the shag carpeted floor. Regaining my feet and my jilted composure, another round of beers was requested and the momentary silence created by the Bruce Lee maneuver was quickly replaced by the jeers and laughter of the party goers.

Opening the back door, the chilly night air felt soothing against my perspiring skin. As I looked up into the night sky, I was greeted by millions of twinkling stars. The party was going quite well, the walls of Louie's' house swelled with teenage kids, girls dressed in seductive outfits, while the boys played it cool. I was cooling myself down for round two of Dance Fever when I heard the squeak of the back door being opened. Out came Bob and Rod, we talked for a few minutes, while smoking and sipping on our bottles of beer. Across from the house was the red and white trimmed barn. It was a typical barn of the Area. It had two floors, the first floor was where the bovines came for their milking sessions and the second floor, was the hay mow. It was where the baled hay was kept.

On the second floor, the hay mow's big double doors faced the road and on this particular night, the moon hung full and bright. As we quietly discussed the nights festivities, someone walked up and planted a piece of information that was about to change the course of our evening.

Rumor was, that a friend of ours, had successfully seduced a girl, the Dentists daughter if I remember, and currently was attempting to romanticize her in the hay mow. Being young and of an impetuous nature, we quickly decided that this piece of information required a visual verification.

Gathering outside the side door of the barn's first floor, we excitedly discussed our plan of attack. Like well-trained navy seals, we formed a single column and then proceeded with our ingress into the building. In the dark, we paused long enough to allow our night vision to improve and to stifle the giggling that someone had started, after a minute or two, we regained our military composure and proceeded in single file across the darkened concrete floor of the barn.

Louie was on point, with his intimate knowledge of the barn's layout, it was imperative that he led, it decreased the chance of us committing any noise violations. As we moved gracefully and noiseless across the lime covered concrete floor, our hearts began to thump wildly as we approached the stairs that led to the second floor of the barn.

With the stealth of ninjas', we quickly and quietly climbed the stairs and were now on the same level as our two supposed love birds. Moving slowly, we crouched one behind the other and as we inched closer, the bright moon light clearly illuminated the surrounding area. Stopping suddenly, we now saw two silhouetted shapes, laying upon the soft hay, in front of the open doors. We could clearly hear the moans and groans of two people in the midst of foreplay.

Gathering our wits and working hard at controlling our laughter, we moved ever closer. As we approached to within feet of the two love birds, we could now see the illuminated images of Mark and his partner. Stopping, we knelt quietly upon the yellow hay covered floor, watching intently as the two played the teenage game of hugs and kisses. When, suddenly, Mark lifted up his head and rolled onto his right side, without saying a word his hand moved towards the button that was holding up her halter top. With the flick of his wrist, the halter top slid slowly down her ribs and as the moonlight illuminated her now exposed breasts someone in our group suddenly shouted out "O my God", in a split-second, she began screaming and began to wildly search for her halter top while flinging Mark off to one side.

In the blink of an eye, we were up and running, laughing vigorously inside the dark confines of the barns second floor. Bob was directly in front of me and as we were running, he suddenly disappeared. I mean one moment he was right in front of me and the next moment, poof he was gone. Out of reflex, I slammed on the brakes while the others quickly piled up against me. With my toes on the edge of an open trap door, that was used to throw bales of hay from the second floor to the first, I stood frozen in fear, staring into the gaping hole. Terror now coursed through me as I tried to imagine the fate of our friend. It registered grimly that he had plunged from the second floor to the hard concrete slab below. We moved quickly to reach him and to provide any feeble first aid that we could muster.

But to our great relief Bob was standing firmly upon his feet and was assuring us that he was just fine. As we exited the barn, we could still hear the distant commotion coming from the hay mow above us. Feeling relieved, we retreated back to the house and continued to party into the wee hours of the morning.

To this day I still think Bob woke up the next morning a bit on the sore and painful side. And to Mark and his companion we apologize for the romantic interruptus, but damn if we had to do it all over again, we would do it in a heart-beat. Thanks to my great high school friends for all the good times, looking back those were some of the best days of our lives.

• • • •• • • • ••

The sunlight glared against the dirt-streaked window. I squinted my eyes, against the bright onslaught The sudden metallic ringing of the school bell startled me, "now don't forget to read chapter three for tomorrows discussion", the English teacher shouted above the din. Walking out into the hallway during class changes was like trying to maneuver down a crowded New York City Street at rush hour. I started jogging towards my locker, my next class was on the adjacent side of the school and I didn't want to be late.

As I turned the corner, a grim scene befell my hazel eyes, a bully had my lightweight friend Joe up against his locker, "hey, what the hell is going on", I shouted, throwing my English literature books upon the tiled floor. Grabbing the attacker; I quickly turned the tables upon him. Using my right forearm; I firmly planted it against his windpipe, with my face mere inches away. "And if I ever see you picking on Joe again, you will surely rue the day", I finished with. And to punctuate my meaning, I spun him sideways and planted my foot tripping him. His momentum carried him forward, crashing him onto the floor with a loud thud. I turned to Joe as the bully fled the scene and asked, "are you all right", he smiled and then nodded, As I walked away, he suddenly found his voice and shouted, "my house at seven tonight, "sure, I'll be their Joe", I shouted back over my shoulder.

As I turned the corner, the shrill sound of the school bell announced that the next set of classes had just begun, "damnit", I muttered, "I see another hour of detention in my future", I exclaimed, as I ran towards the now closed door of my math class.

Hopping down the basement stairs, clearing two at a time and with three steps left, I launched myself and landed catlike onto the green concrete floor. Turning left at the landing, I walked into the finished portion of the basement and started shuffling through the stack of albums laying next to the record player that my sister, and I shared. Towards the bottom of the stack, I found the object of my musical desire, the Beatles White album. After, pulling the glossy vinyl record from its white cover, I carefully placed it upon the turntable and turned up the volume.

Sitting by the bar, I lit a pall mall cigarette and listened intently to the raspy sound of Dear Prudence. By the time the song While my Guitar Gently Weeps was resonating off the basement walls, I was laid out upon the dusty couch. Awaiting the delicious vittles my dad was preparing

[124]

upstairs. But, without warning, the seductive mistress of dreams applied her magic and within seconds, I fell fast asleep. I was suddenly awakened by the loud deep voice of my father, "Bob, suppers ready", he shouted. Shaking off the tentacles of the dream weaver, I staggered towards the stairway and the tantalizing aroma of a perfectly finished beef roast.

The brisk fall temperatures, as I began my two-mile journey to Joe's house, felt invigorating. The wonderful, sweet smell of burning leaves filled the town's atmosphere as households were finishing up the last of their yard work. Jack Frost was already applying his artistic skills and the chilly air reminded us that the soft snows of winter were just around the corner.

Walking up the bridge, the smells of food mingling with the sounds of patrons, enjoying their chosen establishments, became more and more distinct. As I waited at the stop and go lights, at the top of the main street bridge, a car passed by, it's windows open, it's interior bristling with the squeals and jeers of young kids searching for their nightly adventure. Just four more blocks and my long walk would be over, I pulled up my jackets collar to shield against the cool night and then briskly crossed the street,

Standing at the door, the sounds of Joe and his brothers engaged in a robust conversation about dishwashing made me smile, Joe, for his age, was a bit on the petite side, but he could stand his ground with the best of us and his superior intelligence made up any lacking of physical stature. I remember an incident during the summer, a bunch of us had gathered at a nearby park, not far from Joe's house, to play a game of baseball. Joe not being the athletic type, decided that a tall shade tree and a good book was far more satisfying than playing America's favorite pastime.

As the game progressed, I don't recall who, but someone applied a large amount of wood to a fast pitch and as we watched the magnificent trajectory of that home run, it became apparent that its course seemed to be on a direct path towards Joe, who was comfortably stretched out under a tall, green shade tree. As our various voices of warning was finally heard, he had just enough time to look up as the ball impacted him squarely in the eye. What a shiner, it was one of the biggest and brightest black eyes that I have ever seen.

After receiving no response from my first announcement, I knocked even louder on the door to be heard above the raucous din that was going on inside. Suddenly, a brief moment of silence and then the sound of feet rapidly approaching the door. As the door flung open, I saw Eric standing on the threshold smiling. "Can I help you sir", he said, "is Joe home you little shit", I responded laughing. "Why sure, come on in", he retorted.

As I entered the living room, I saw Joe's dad sitting in his worn but comfortable easy chair, reading the latest edition of the Kaukauna Times. I heard the wrinkling of paper as he turned a page and without looking up, he said, "Hi Bob, how are you", in a monotone voice, "I'm doing fine Mr. Jacobson", I exclaimed. An awkward moment of silence followed as I searched for something more substantial. Abruptly, I saw Joe bounding down the stairs, a sigh of relieve escaped my lips, "hey Zeke, thanks for showing up, come on out to the garage I have some work to do", he said.

The last reds of the evening sky greeted our egress as we walked the short distance to the garage. Joe reached down and opened the large garage door. I have to admit, every time I looked inside, I was amazed as if it was the first time. From front to back, the interior space was loaded with machines, pinball machines, jukeboxes, foosball tables, I watched fascinated as Joe was making repairs on a pinball machine. The number of wires threaded from one component to another was mind boggling, but he carefully followed their course and made the necessary repairs. My role was to provide comedic relief and to boost his ego by reminding him how good he was on the complicated stuff. After a few hours of watching the repair maestro in action and me holding up the wall, Joe declared mission accomplished and announced it was time to head downtown. Standing on the driveway, I watched Joe turn off the lights, shut the garage door and securely lock it. Turning around he smiled and said, "are you ready", "Joe, I was born ready", I responded with a grin. Walking down his driveway, we took a left and headed toward his parents' pool hall which was located on Wisconsin Avenue.

The pool hall was located next to Tommy G's, and as we walked up the street, the camaraderie and jubilation coming from that establishment was intoxicating. The pool hall was aged, with large windows lining the front, allowing passerby's the ability to watch the events taking place inside. Most of the patrons were older males and with most pool halls, it was a place where young males could test their testosterone levels by challenging friends or strangers to a game of billiards, usually involving money.

My heart beat a little faster as I, an eighth grader, entered the domain of the older more dominant males, I stuck close to the shirttails of my friend. "Hey Joe is that your new girlfriend", said one of the larger menacing pool players, "yep, what are yak, jealous", was his response. The male in the sleeveless denim jacket pulled hard on his cigarette and with a steely glint in his eye, grinned, "ya, good one Joe". Expelling a loud sigh of relief, I followed Joe as we entered the kitchen area of the establishment. The short order cook, was placing paddies of beef upon the hot flat grill, while also keeping an eye on the fryer as it bubbled and spat with a fresh load of French fries. The one menu item that I craved every time I was in the Pool Hall, was a hot batch of French fries served up with a large batch of tartar sauce.

After Joe examined the cash register and placed a few rolls of quarters into it, we headed for the basement to retrieve some necessary supplies. As we started back up the stairs, the room above us erupted into loud shouts, fearing a fight over a lost pool game, we sprinted up the remaining stairs to assess the situation.

Upon re-entering the first floor of the building, an acrid cloud of smoke assaulted our nostrils and set about burning our eyes. A grease fire had started in the kitchen and was quickly getting out of control. Joe rushed into the kitchen to help extinguish the fire as I stood fearfully spellbound, watching the red and orange tongues of flames rapidly consume the surrounding materials. Within minutes, the fire spread from the grill to the surrounding walls, the people in the kitchen attempting to halt it's spread, abandoned their efforts and fled by jumping over the counter and running for the safety of the street.

As the life-threatening black smoke grew more dense and wide spread, I covered my mouth with my hands and in a half crouch, ran for my life. As we stood across the street, the interior of the building was completely obscured by the thick, hot, black smoke. The sounds of crackling wood and shattering windows could now be clearly heard as throngs of people from nearby businesses flooded into the streets.

The ear shattering sirens of the fire trucks pierced the air as the head of the fire monster hissed and roared until it shot into the dark night, rising far above the rooftop. I stood dumbstruck as I watched the anguish in Joes face as his family's source of income was evaporating into the flame lit sky.

As the last fire truck rolled up their hoses and slowly pulled away. We gingerly entered the remains of the building. The smell of smoke was almost overwhelming as Joe and his family assessed the damage. The once vibrant business was now reduced to blackened walls and shattered windows. I quietly gave my condolences to the family, exited the building and headed for the quiet safety of my home.

As the weeks turned into months, the trauma of that night faded quietly away. Replaced by the trials and tribulations of living through puberty. As I was standing at my locker, placing my textbooks into their bimetal home for the weekend, Joe approached and excitedly exclaimed, "are you coming to the grand opening of the new pool hall", "man I had totally forgot about the pool hall, sure, what time" I said. "Come by Saturday morning and I'll give you the grand tour", he responded.

We entered the business through the back door, seeing it wasn't open to the public quite yet, at the turn of the key and the click of the lock, Joe smiled and said, "man wait until you see this place".

The smell of new carpet and fresh paint had replaced the smell of destruction, and as we entered into the main area, I stopped in my tracks, amazed at the beautiful transformation, gone was the aged and outdated flooring and wall coverings. Replaced by a fashionably new and a highly appealing décor. The shiny chromed pin ball machines glistened in the new overhead lighting and instead of pool tables dominating the space, it now sported a myriad of exciting new gaming devices while the newly rebuilt kitchen contained a new fire extinguishing system to prevent any future tragic mishaps.

The place was absolutely beautiful, "hey joe do you mind if I play some pinball", I asked, "be my guest Bob, you remember how to turn them on right", "yep, I sure do", I replied back. I reached around the back of the machine, found the tiny lever switch and proceeded to turn it up. As I watched the electronics of this quarter gobbling device spring to life, a feeling of pure happiness flowed through my body, a tragic moment of time for a close friend was now transformed into a new future of hope and prosperity.

I rapidly manipulated the paddles a few times, then I pulled back upon the spring-loaded lever and let it go. I watched in total concentration as the round, steel ball began its journey through the maze of bells, bumpers and flashing contacts and as the last ball of the game sped past my paddles, I dug my hand into my tight well-worn blue jeans and fished around for another quarter, "hey joe, you got change for a five", I hollered. "No problem" was his response. "How do you like the new place", he shouted. "I love it", I hollered back", "but it's sure going to cost me a small fortune in allowances", I quietly said to myself.

"By the way Joe, what name are you giving the new pool hall", I asked. "We are going the call it the Phoenix ", he replied back. "The Phoenix, what's that", I answered back, "it's a mythical creature, a bird, that when it dies, it bursts into flames and is consumed down to ashes. And then a new bird arises out those ashes", he exclaimed. Wow, that I thought was the perfect name, the Phoenix.

[128]

• •• • • •• •••• • •• • • •

The warm morning sun felt good as I sat on the porch watching my neighborhood slowly come to life. The song birds filled the air with their harmonic melodies and the squirrels diligently searched the lawn for any buried treasures left over from last year's harvest. Looking up I spotted Tom crossing the street and moving towards my location. "Good morning, Tom", I expressed as he climbed onto the concrete porch and sat down quietly next to me. "Morning Bob" was his return response. We then spent the next twenty minutes talking about what most ten-year old boys discuss, what we did yesterday and what might be on the agenda for today. Toms face contorted into a look of apathy when my sad joke fell upon his ears and then giggled as he articulated his concern for my lack of a comedic touch.

It wasn't long before we heard the sound of rubber soled sneakers flapping noisily against the concrete sidewalk. Looking up we spotted another friend approaching and as Mark jumped up onto the porch Tom and I broke, simultaneously into a chorus of good mornings. While Mark searched for a more comfortable seat, the discussion of the day's possible events began to unfold. Tom's suggestion was to complete the underground fort we had started in the empty wood lot across from Dick's Drive In. Mark and I responded, it was going to be way to hot and humid to be digging out the remainder of the fort. We sat in silence for the next few minutes softly observing the unfolding of the new day.

The quiet of the moment was shattered as I heard my mom loudly call out my name, "I'll be right there", I hollered back. "Sorry guys we'll have to meet later, I've got my Saturday morning chores to get done". With a groan of disappointment, I lifted myself up and into the awakening house.

My last chore of that morning was to clean my room and I was becoming more animated knowing my labors would soon be put behind me. As I stepped on the off switch, a smile spread swiftly across my face, that is until my mom's voice rang out, "Bob, make sure you clean under the bed this time", "Damn", I muttered as the vacuum cleaner noisily sprang back to life.

The cold gulp of milk felt refreshing as it cascaded down my throat and with a sigh of satisfaction, I delved hungrily into my bologna, cheese and mayo sandwich "Hey mom that was a great sandwich" I said after the last tasty morsel had taken its journey. As I was getting up from the yellow padded kitchen chair, I heard a persistent knock at the back door. "I'll get it", I hollered. I took off running down the hallway. Approaching the back door, I braked hard. Losing my balance I fell towards the hardwood floor, thrusting out my left hand, I prevented my nose from making a hard and painful landing.

Walking to the back door, I saw Norman standing patiently, waiting for my arrival. "Hi Norm, what's up" I said. "I was wondering if you wanted to go to the pool today", he responded. "I talked to the other guys and they all agreed to go", he continued. Norman wiped his nose and stared down at his feet, waiting for my reply. Pondering the possibility for a few seconds I said, "absolutely I'll go, just let me know what time" "Be ready in about thirty minutes "he hollered as he jumped off the back porch.

Running to my room I hollered, 'Mom I am going to the pool with the guys, is that all right", without waiting for a response I began to dig through my dresser drawer looking for my brightly colored swim suit. Her response was somewhat faint and muffled, "alright, just make sure your back by supper and ask your dad for some money for the food shack, don't want ya starving". I continued ransacking my dresser drawer and then with a shout of triumph, I lifted my bathing suit out and slammed the drawer shut. Turning my attention upon my dad, I ran down the hall and quickly opened the screeching back door and leapt off the porch.

The sound of the high-pitched skill saw easily marked his location. I waited somewhat impatiently for him to finish his task and when I saw my opening "hey dad", I said with the screech of the saw still buzzing in my ears, "mom said I could go to the pool and I was to ask you for some money for the food shack". He stared at me quietly for a few moments, shook his head and reached for his wallet. As he was handing me a fresh one dollar bill, he paused and said, "now remember son I expect you to have the grass cut by tomorrow", "sure dad", I responded, but as my hand was stretched out in midair he looked down at me with an intense gaze and said, "Bob repeat what I just said", "Uh, cut the grass tomorrow", I exclaimed. I felt the stiff paper of the dollar bill touch my fingers and like the reflex of an alligator, I quickly clamped down and left before he had a chance to reconsider his decision.

Upon reaching my bedroom, I seized my Bahama style swim suit and quickly headed towards the bathroom, where I obtained a very important piece of equipment, my towel.

As I exited the house, I spotted, laying askew upon the grass, my dingy, paint chipped black Huffy. A twenty-six-inch single speed beauty, that has seen more combat than most war veterans. Kneeling down, I folded the bath towel in half, I then placed my swim suit onto the towel and rolled it up forming a cylinder shape. Straddling the bike, I wedged the rolled towel tightly between the top tube and the secondary tube. This allowed me to transport my bathing suit without the use of my hands, which is why that towel is an important piece of equipment.

Next, I jumped onto the bike seat and pushed hard upon the upright pedal; the bike slowly started to roll and then with each successive hard turn of the crank, the bike began to pick up speed and as I hit the end of the driveway, my mechanical steed was rolling smoothly along. I could see my gang of friends just ahead of me, each on their own prized velocipede, "hey guys wait for me", I shouted and then sprinted to catch up.

The ride to the pool with the gang was always in the form of a race, each of us taking turns sprinting to get to the head of the pack. If we decided not to take the long way around, we would head for Cutlers Hill.

Cutlers Hill was an old access road composed of dirt and gravel, what it was used for long ago, I have no clue. But currently, it was closed off to traffic by a heavy chrome plated barrier. You entered on the left side; there was a path just big enough for a single rider to pass through. At the top, there was a small flat spot, the rest of the road was very steep, I mean you can't keep your feet on the pedals steep.

After we had all passed through; we lined up and raced down that road. Upon reaching the bottom you had a choice to make; you could apply your brakes with all the force you could muster and make a hard left onto the railroads access road or you remained straight ahead and followed a narrow dirt path through tall grass that terminated at a set of three railroad tracks. Either way from there, it was a short ride to the glimmering pool.

Upon reaching the pool, we raced across the sloped lawn and joined the long, slithering line of kids impatiently waiting for their entry. We passed the time talking quietly amongst ourselves and visually inspecting each new arrival. As we passed through the front doors, well-tanned teenagers dressed in skimpy bathing suits, accepted our money and handed each of us a metal basket which housed our clothing.

The heavy concrete block walls of the dressing room bounced the myriads of screams, laughter and loud conversations around and then mixed them into an unintelligible globe of noise. The stained concrete floors near the showers were constantly wet and I almost slipped as I walked towards the long, hard surfaced benches used for changing. The open aired dressing room held no privacy, so you undressed quickly.

Walking to the shallow end of the pool, I dipped my foot into its cold water, man it didn't matter the month or the time of day, that water always raised goose bumps. I had to decide between the slow agonizing method or the all at once method. I decided on the later. Taking a deep breath, I jumped in. The initial shock took my breath away and made my scalp feel as if it suddenly shrunk down two sizes.

As I was attempting to locate my friends, a face suddenly appeared from the pools depths and before I could utter a sound, two hands unceremoniously pushed me towards the bottom. Unable to take a deep breath, it wasn't long before the feeling of suffocation overwhelmed me. The trick to escape was to swim towards the bottom and then push up and away.

As my head broke the surface, I located the position of my prankster, as he was now trying to escape unseen by swimming periodically under water. I swam as fast as I could and proceeded to cut him off at the pass. As he slowly raised his head I pounced quickly and decisively pushing him back down under the water. After he came back up, I couldn't help but laugh and feel a bit sorry for him as he spit and sputtered for a lung full of air. "Damnit Bob you could have drowned me", he cried. Swimming backwards, I called back, "turn arounds a bitch isn't it", we then both laughed and started our search amongst the many wet and bobbing heads for the rest of our friends.

Mark was standing behind me in the four-foot section of the pool, diving under, I reached up and grabbed his cold shriveled hands as Mark proceeded to climb up upon my shoulders. I wiped the water from my face and instantly heard Mark say "Bob, turn to the right", as I turned right, Randy and Norman speedily engaged us, I could feel Norman pulling Mark hard to the left and quickly I adjusted my footing to keep our balance, and immediately we were pulled in the opposite direction. The coup de grace came when the opposing team was able to pull Mark forward which left me unable to correct our center of gravity, his weight pushed us deep into the pool's depths. As we surfaced, we saw Randy and Norman were now grappling with Tom and Steve, in a game of water jousting. As the victors raised their hands in triumph, we defeated ones saddled up for round two.

Towards the end of the day, I was sitting on the edge of the pool feeling rather disappointed. Most of my friends had moved on to the deep end and were enjoying the acrobatics of the diving boards. I couldn't cross over that line because I did not possess the required pass that demonstrated my swimming prowess. To earn that badge of honor one must swim, non-stop, from one side of the pool and then back again, while the lifeguard monitored your success or failure.

Mark came over and quietly sat down next to me, "Bob, go ahead and try it again, this time might be the one", he said. "I don't know Mark" I replied. "You'll never get it if you don't try", he exclaimed. "Oh right, I'll try Mark", I said. I stood up from the edge of the pool and walked over to the lifeguard sitting atop his tower. "Sir, I am ready to take my test". Ignoring me, he suddenly stood up and blew into his silver whistle, the nostrils of his zinc coated nose flared as he shouted loudly to be heard above the din. As he sat back down, I shouted, "hey I would like to take my deep-water test now". He turned in his seat and stared down at me, "so you think your ready uh", he said removing his sunglasses. "I do believe I am", I replied back. "Okay let me know when you're ready", he responded. I looked at Mark, he smiled and gave me the thumbs up.

I looked across the pool, the distance seemed dauntingly too far. After my last failed attempt, an older friend of mine had suggested a new strategy, "next time", he said, "swim under water for as long as you can and then swim back as fast as you can". As I stood looking down into the pool's depths, I flapped my arms across my chest, took a deep breath and dove in.

I swam hard under water, my lungs burning, my brain screaming for more oxygen. When I surfaced, I was amazed that I was just a few feet from the opposite side of the pool, I started my free style technique, I touched the side of the pool, and immediately turned and started the swim back. I felt the same feeling of defeat as my legs and arms grew heavy from the exertion, I peeked ahead and saw I was about fifteen feet from the finish line and as my brain screamed stop, I willed my tired body forward.

My hand slammed painfully into the side of the pool. I desperately searched for a hand hold or else I felt I would sink to the bottom of the pool. I was tired, I didn't believe I could have swam another stroke and as I clung to the edge, feeling entirely spent. I saw Mark kneeling over the edge and felt him slapping me on the back. I had done it. I had earned my right to the deep end of the pool

The accomplishment began to slowly creep into my mind; I now had the power to cross over and join the throngs of other kids at the privileged end of the pool. I walked with pride to the counter and presented my water spotted slip of paper entitling me to the coveted patch. I stood staring at the cloth patch; it had the year stamped on it. With pride, I pinned it to my bathing suit. and joined my friends on the high dive. The day never felt better.

Staring up at the ladder of the high dive, it appeared to extend up into the heavens. The high dive was a rite of courage for kids, the top of the platform was ten feet off the ground, its ladder stretched straight up. Just climbing it produced cold, clammy hands, it made your head swim.

The climb seemed to last forever and as I stepped onto the platform, I stood still, almost paralyzed. One false move and they would be hosing your remains off the concrete below. You felt the wind pushing on you but stretching out in front was an amazing panoramic view. I gingerly walked out, mindful not to fall off the side and onto the hard concrete below.

As my toes reached the end of the board, I looked down, I felt the breeze buffeting my face, I saw bobbing faces below, encouraging you to jump. There was no backing down, a string of kids now waited on the ladder, screaming at you to jump, the only exit was forward and through a deep column of air. I don't remember jumping off the board, but the fall felt forever, until suddenly, the surface of the water rushed up and pulled you into its icy grip.

The exhilaration I felt was beyond belief; I had passed the test of courage. From that moment on, the high dive lost most if it's initial terror, instead it became the premiere object of our pool passions. Performing cannon ball contests, learning the art and grace of a back dive or feeling the gravity defying effects of a somersault. I was no longer a child relegated to the baby pool or to the shallow end, but with my patch proudly displayed, I was as big as any other kid or teenager that could play beyond the rope.

As the afternoon sun began its slide towards the horizon, we gathered at the edge of the pool, talking and laughing about the day's events. We had one traditional task yet to perform before we made our way towards the dressing room, that task was to harass the life guards. In our defense, they, the lift guards, at times, would openly mock us regarding our juvenile state of development.

We lined up at the low board which was conveniently located near a life guard tower. The devious plan was to, as rapidly as we could, launch ourselves off the spring board, towards the tower, drenching the unsuspecting life guard with an icy cold splash. Being last in line, I was blessed with witnessing the robust effects of our attack, by the time I was exiting the pool, the life guard was a red faced, water dripping, cussing, transformed image of itself. The last sentence usually uttered, understandably, was "And now, please remove yourself from the facility", which we were in the act of doing anyway.

Standing at the counter with blue lips and shriveled skin, we handed in our oversized diaper pins for the contents of its corresponding basket, hopefully containing our clothes and not someone else's, and then head into the raucous din of the dressing room.

While waiting outside for the remainder of our group to exit, we would huddle into a loose circle, mostly quiet, as the feeling of exhaustion began to overtake you. The conversation, as we walked towards the food shack, was almost always concentrated on, "okay what are you getting today", the plethora of candy choices at that food shack could rival any modern chain store of today. The decision was always difficult but with a choice in hand, we would retreat to the top of the hill, under the shade trees and silently enjoy our treats while observing the kids still splashing and playing in the pool's icy depths. The ensuing ride home was quiet and slow, at times, turning the crank took the remainder of any energy you had left. But at last home was reached and the bike once again, lay askew upon the grass. and as I opened the shrieking back door I yelled, "hey mom, what's for supper".

．．．．．． ．． ．． ． ． ．．． ． ．

The high-pitched tweets and clicks of a variety of colorful songs from birds engaged in their daily routines greeted my ears, rolling over, I pulled the pillow over my head. Instantly, I was in a state of purgatory, the world that lies between consciousness and dream land and now that veil of sleep was once again, slowly spreading across the recesses of my brain. A shrill voice suddenly yanked me out of its blissful grasp. "Hey wake up Bob, dad wants you to cut the grass this morning" my sister yelled into my ear. "Damn, sis don't you know how to knock" I muttered angrily. "I could, but it sure as hell wouldn't be as much fun", she said with a sadistic grin. As she slammed the door for emphasis, I rolled over and sat up. The vivid images of my dreams were now quickly fading. Reaching up, I rubbed the encrusted rheum from the corners of my eyes and lit up a cigarette and as the nicotine began to swiftly spread through my circulatory system, the mornings state of purgatory was promptly being chased back into its spiritual realm.

The maple-stained hard wood floors, even though it was summer, still felt cool upon the soles of my calloused feet. The smell of brewing coffee hung sweet and heavy in the hallway as I approached the kitchen. The sudden rustling of a newspaper being read meant my dad was already at the kitchen table, "morning pop" I said as I entered the room. "Did Gail deliver my message this morning", he said with a smile. "Loud and clear", I answered back.

As I walked around the yellow veneered chair, I paused and kissed him upon the top of his Vitalis infused hair. Reaching for a white napkin I laughed and said, "hey pops when are you going to change that oil". "Very funny", my dad retorted. "Now remember Bob, I want that lawn done before I get home from work today", he said in a firm tone.

My dad hardly ever raised his voice, but over the years I have come to learn that what dad said, dad meant, he never, ever failed to deliver any consequences. "You bet pops" I said as I turned to retrieve the cold bottle of milk

After rummaging through the cupboard, I found my favorite cereal bowl, it was used for the consumption of my favorite, sugar coated, multi colored, balls of baked corn, a confection affectionately known as Captain Crunch.

As my teeth sumptuously ground those tasty confections into a swallowable mass, I quietly pondered my days activities. The first task had already been assigned, cut the lush green grass, check, well that's seems to be the current digestible list, which meant the rest of the day was wide open for any adventures that would meander my way.

The early morning sun was hanging low on the horizon. It felt unusually hot and small rivulets of sweat began to course down my body. I groaned as I stopped to wipe the stinging sweat from my red irritated eyes. The large backyard seemed to stretch on for miles. Feeling the heat, I shook my head and took a swig from my warm can of Pepsi. Determined to finish the mission, I plodded on.

After the last swath of grass was clipped, I turned off the lawn mower and watched as it sputtered and shook itself to a stop. After two hours of sweat induced work, I had completed my first task, the lawn was cut.

Standing and gazing upon my accomplishment, I suddenly heard the metallic ring of our lime green telephone. Reacting quickly, I pushed the lawn mower into the garage and then sprinted up the concrete steps of the back porch. I entered the house and ran to the still ringing phone; breathing hard I picked up the receiver and said, "hello, Zierler's mortuary, you stab em, we slab em", that was my favorite greeting and as a grin began to spread across my face; I heard the response, "do you have bud in a can" as hushed giggles could now be heard in the background. I couldn't believe it; I was being phone pranked. Unfortunately, for these young pranksters, a year long bout with a phone stalker concerning my younger sister had brought about a rather effective solution. After months of police reports and requests for phone surveillance, a simple resolution presented itself, during a conversation with a friend who had endured the same misery. The resolution came in the form of compressed air, yes folks an air horn.

Reaching up to the top of the refrigerator, I retrieved the brightly-painted air horn and then spoke clearly into the phone, "why yes we do have bud in a can" and as I heard "well then", I pulled the phone from my ear, placed the air horn against the transmitter and let out a long, loud blast of compressed air. As I placed the receiver back upon the wall mount, I heard the shrill screams coming from the prankster. Smiling, I said grinning, "paybacks a bitch"

The rest of the day was a common list of summer activities. The rest of the 18th street gang had now gathered and were in the street playing a game called five hundred. You designated a batter who would hit popups while the rest of us kids pushed, pulled and tripped each other to snare the baseball before it hit the ground. The lucky recipient would be awarded a certain number of points and the kid who acquired the first total of five hundred points was the winner and became the next designated batter.

The next designated stop was the underground fort. Inside that homemade enclosure, we had one playboy magazine, a pack of cigarettes with matches and a superman comic book. After we bailed out the water, from a recent rain storm, we coughed and laughed as we shared a cigarette while passing around the dog-eared playboy magazine.

It was at the pool where I met my friend Ray and after a few episodes of cannon ball contests and death-defying dives consisting of forward and backward somersaults with some gainers thrown in, we left the chlorinated waters of the pool and headed for the candy shack that sat below the tree lined hillside. As we enjoyed our delicious treats, Ray asked if I wanted to go to his house, "sure", I said, I loved his parents, they were, at times, as much my parents as my real parents were.

Walking up to the deciduous trees along the top of the hill, we quietly sat and watched the kids as they played rambunctious in the pool below. Sitting in the shade, as the breeze caressed my body, which helped to beat back the summer heat and it wasn't long before I slowly closed my eyes and fell fast asleep.

As I entered the living room, Richie, Rays brother looked up and called out, "hey Zeke" and promptly stood up and embraced me in a sincere hug. As we sat in the kitchen discussing important matters, such as girls, a new subject was suddenly broached, a friend had recently experienced a bit of trauma involving a police officer. I don't recall the motive for what was being planned but the prank that our friend was now laying out was pure genius. As we discussed the details, the tantalizing smell of cooking sausages was becoming too much to bear. We put aside our plans and then akin to a pack of coyotes on a fresh road kill, we dove into that platter of pigs in a blanket.

The summer sun was now slowly fading and the days temperature was, happily, dialed down a few degrees. Only the sound of our rubber soled sneakers along with our hushed voices marked our passage. Our final destination was a small walk space between two buildings located on East Second Street. As we neared our destination, our hearts beat wildly, our bodies tingled, heightened senses that only adrenaline can produce.

We attempted to act normally as we approached the small walkway, as if others could sense our intentions. Stopping we stared into the dark passage way, taking turns cautiously peering down its narrow and darkened portal. The space was barely wide enough for a single large adult and with the prank requiring no witnesses, that dark and narrow passage provided the perfect environment from which to execute our plan. We patiently waited for the street traffic to pass by and then we slipped, quietly, into the mouth of that dimly lit passage.

Even though outside the passage, the light of day provided a bright field of view, the narrow confines of the passage combined with the tall structures proceeded to block out most of the sunlight. We talked in hushed whispers as we went through the plan for a final time. Nodding our heads in agreement, Cud fished out the soft coil of rope from inside of his sweat dampened shirt. We waited quietly for the shade of the evening before executing our prank.

As evening approached, the shadows began to grow long and narrow, Cud eased out of our hiding place and stepped out into the alley. Ensuring that the coast was clear, he quickly walked to the telephone pole located directly across from our location. Cud quickly began to calculate the correct height for the rope and proceeded to tie a secure knot, and then swiftly ran back to our hiding spot.

As he ran back, I saw the smile spread across his face, we were ready. Like athletes waiting for the start of a sporting event, we felt the tension, our bodies coiled, ready for action. In the distance, the faint growl of a motorbike, we felt it, it was kickoff time.

The sound of a three wheeled motorcycle moving towards us, alerted us to his presence. A certain police officer was making his rounds, checking doors and looking for criminal activity. Cud had staked out his routine for the past week, he patrolled this alleyway every evening, at the same time, as precise as a Swiss watch. The motorcycles engine uttered a low growling pulse as he waited for traffic to clear and then unsuspecting, he turned into the alley.

As he made his way, our muscles coiled, our bodies trembled as we anticipated the timing. Like a pride of lions, we crouched, with muscles tense, we waited for the right moment to spring and then suddenly Cud yelled, PULL. The rope that lay soft upon the ground quickly snapped into a tight barrier of nylon. The motorcycle passed under the tight rope and caught the unsuspecting officer just above the windshield and across his chest. And in slow motion, the officer now unseated, hung suspended in midair, in the same sitting position as if he was still mounted, and then as gravity kicked in, he landed hard onto the alleyway.

In the blink of an eye, we were running down the passage laughing so hard tears semi blinded us and just before we exited, we heard a barrage of curses and in his rage, he pulled his revolver and emptied it into the darkening summer sky.

We ran back until our lungs burned and our legs felt like lead. We sat for a few hours expecting to hear the sound of sirens or the baying of tracking dogs, as they hunted down the dastardly culprits, but as the evening turned into night, the sound of crickets and tree frogs were the only sound that punctuated the night. I soon said my good byes and headed towards the safety of my awaiting home.

• • • •• • ••• ••• •• • • •• •• •

I had just spent the last four weeks watching the fall fairy turn the summer shimmering green leaves into their brilliant awe-inspiring fall colors. I was starting to feel fairly despondent, my left leg had been severely broken, the tibia and fibula required plates and screws and my left ankle had been completely dislocated. And to top it off, I had to have pins inserted into my right thumb to re-attach that appendage back onto the rest of my hand. With a cast up to my elbow on my right arm and a full-length cast encasing my left leg I was now firmly planted upon the proverbial pity pot and my negativity was fertilizing those emotions on a daily basis.

My sister Gail and her boyfriend, no neck Chuck, had just picked me up from the medical center and was transporting my sorry carcass back home. As the familiar landscape flowed across the surface of my retinas, I reached into my pocket and pulled out a fresh cigarette from the crumpled pack and as the blue white smoke circled lazily around my head I pondered the bleak reality of my now altered future.

That football scholarship I was anticipating was now evaporating as quickly as the dry paper on my lit cigarette, I could feel the beginning of a tear develop as I rolled down the car window and flipped the long grey ash into the brisk fall air.

The harmonic beat of Crosby, Stills, Nash and Young pulsated through the house as I sat in my wheelchair staring longingly at the social activities of my fellow neighbors. My world now consisted of sponge baths, soap operas and ash trays overflowing with cigarette butts. I can't say I was depressed, but if my lower lip hung any lower it was now dangerously close to being ripped off by the vacuum cleaner as my mom cleaned the carpet.

As another wave of self-defeating pity was beginning to splash against my psyche, the metallic ringing of the telephone suddenly interrupted its insidious intent. Spinning the wheel chair around, I pushed hard against its rubber wheels. I could already hear the rhythmic beat of my older sister's feet as she dashed to answer the phone. Just as she raised her hand to intercept it, I edged my wheel chair between her and the intended objective and with a satisfying sneer I reached up and removed the lime green hand set from its wall mount. "Damnit Bob you could have broken some of my toes with that juvenile behavior of yours", my sister lamented. "Sorry sis", I answered back, "but sadly this is now

[142]

the highlight of my day" I said. And then I gave her my sad puppy eyes and slowly tilted my head to the side, I began to emanate whining sounds. "You're such a shit" she angrily stated and then turned and walked quickly away.

Placing the large hand set to my ear I gave my standard greeting, "hello bob's mortuary, you stab em, we slab em", there was a brief pause on the other end and then to my dismay a familiar voice stuttered out, "damn bob you're
such a shit", immediately the sound track for the twilight zone began to play inside my head. "Hey Ray what's up", I shot back. "I was wondering if your free tonight" he said with a giggle. "I don't know Ray I was scheduled to start salsa dance lessons this evening" I answered back. "Well, there's a party going down tonight and I thought maybe some time out the house would do you some good, are you up for it", he stated. "Absolutely, I am about to go stir crazy if I have to sit looking out the living room window any longer", I responded. "Be ready about eight, I'll come by and pick you up", he excitedly said. As I turned to hang up the phone. With a fresh feeling of exciting anticipation, I wheeled myself into the tight confines of our only family's green painted bathroom and hollered, "Mooooom, I need your help, bobby needs a sponge bath and a shave please".

The red glow of my cigarette softly illuminated the dark living room as I sat, patiently, waiting for my evening's transportation and it wasn't long before the yellow glow of headlights chased the darkness across the room as the car turned into our driveway. The muted sound of voices and laughter could be heard as they approached the back door and as I wheeled my chair around, my sister having had already answered and opened the door, I heard. "Hey Zeke are ya ready", Ray said with a smile, "I was born ready fellas" I answered and after a brief conversation with my mom where they guaranteed my safe return, two of my friends lifted me out of my wheel chair and carried me to the awaiting auto.

The sights and sounds of my home town as we drove towards our destination filled me with a sense of awe and inclusion, you don't really understand how the places and the people in your life fill those nooks and crannies of your existence. They are the ingredients that truly add flavor to our essence and as I watched them flow past the passenger window, I became acutely aware of the methodic beat of We're an American Band that suddenly permeated the car's interior and without missing a beat, our voices joined Mark Farner as he belted out their new tune and as we sang, we laughed. For the first time, in a while, I was starting to feel a sense of normalcy again and as the black and worn radial tires of our metallic steed carried us to our destination, the dark clouds of despair were finally beginning to lift.

The Out-of-Town restaurant was abnormally dark as we turned into its driveway, only the soft glow of candescent lights in the apartment above expressed any human occupancy. A few other cars littered the parking area that normally would be filled on a Saturday night. The owners, as I was told, were taking a well-deserved vacation and their teenage children were left in charge of the property.

As the car rolled to a stop, my compadres exited the vehicle and placed me into the soft padding of my wheel chair. We approaching the side entrance and became quickly aware that the party was not being held on the first floor but instead the party was being held in the living space above the business. Sadly, I stared disappointedly at the rather steep and long flight of steps required to reach the second floor. My newly acquired enthusiasm was now rapidly beginning to diminish. There was no way a boy in a wheel chair was ever to going to ascend that stairway and envelop himself in the warmth and the pleasures of the social experience being played out in the apartment above.

Ray walked over to my side, looked at me and then looked at the long flight of steps, "what's the matter Zeke", he said, "Ray there aint no way I can make it up that stairway", I sadly answered. "Ye of such little faith" he chuckled and promptly Ray and another friend lifted me out of my wheel chair and in a sling fashion, carried me up each step of that barrier while another friend carried my now collapsed wheel chair. As the door opened at the top of the stairs, music loud and clear greeted our auditory canals along with the sounds of a plethora of mingled conversations. As my friends placed me back into my metallic conveyance a chorus of greetings met our excited faces and as the first plastic cup of brewed nectar was placed into my one non-casted hand, the joy of life began to spread throughout my limbs, like the new sap on a warm spring day. This is just what the patient needed I thought as a smile now quickly proliferated across my face.

The party was such a nice piece of psychological medicine, it helped to lift my spirits and to restore my attendance into the pursuit of life, but at last it was time to leave, with a full leg cast and an arm cast now loaded with new well wishes, I eagerly distributed my appreciative hugs and goodbyes and then headed for the door.

There are moments in our lives when a decision really matters, you take one road, the consequences are beautiful and rewarding, you take the other road, those consequences are ugly and punishing, this was one of those moments. With a belly full of beer, I stared down that long steep flight of stairs with a new sense of courage and purpose, those stairs had to be mastered, to be defeated, just like my infirmities. I staggered up out of my two wheeled mode of transportation and then attempted to walk down the steps.

My friends upon seeing my newly found, alcohol fueled, inspiration vigorously tried to dissuade me of my new challenge. Brushing them off, I placed my right leg upon the top step, braced my weight with my useful left arm and swung my fully encased left leg to meet my right leg upon that same step. After a brief waggle, I gathered my balance and proceeded to the next step, right leg down, move the left arm for balance, swing the casted leg to the same step, waggle, regain balance, viola, this didn't seem so hard. Looking up at my compadres, I gave them my see I can do this look and proceeded to the third step. I don't know what part of the sequence I attempted out order, but as I swung my left leg, I suddenly felt myself falling forward. With only one good arm, I could not arrest my out of balance situation and as I fell head first down the stairwell, I felt myself strangely rotating as if trying to complete a somersault. To my amazement instead of landing upon my head or neck, which would have had dire results, paralysis or perhaps even death, I landed a few steps down upon my none flexible casted left leg. Because my left leg couldn't crumple, it instead propelled me forward in a position now akin to a flying superman, but at each forward rotation I somersaulted into a foot first landing position, which would then propel me into another forward rotation, somersault and landing, rinse and repeat.

Now I can positively tell you that I had absolutely no control into the physics of my situation. I definitely was not doing this on purpose; my only explanation relied upon my belief into the realm of the super natural. So, picture an agile, extremely talented gymnast somersaulting across the mat, I was doing this in a now almost vertical orientation. I do recall as I landed at the bottom of the stairs, I felt that my ordeal was about to be over, as I reached out with my good left arm and my casted right arm to stop my forward momentum. To my dismay and to my luck, my forward momentum sent me through the screen door and out into the cold parking lot, the lucky part, I careened through a screen and not a glass enclosed screen door.

As I lay upon the cold hard pavement, I could see my friends running frantically down the stairs, eyes wide in fear and amazement. They knelt quickly by my side and asked If I was hurting anywhere, to my wonderment, I wasn't. After a brief discussion, they gingerly lifted me up and placed me into the back seat of the automobile and raced towards the Kaukauna Hospital emergency room.

Lying upon the cold steel examining table, I couldn't help but giggle over my event, I still could not believe that my fall had not resulted in a more serious condition. My family doctor, Simon Cherkasky, entered the room looking at the x-rays of my left leg and right arm, to make sure the plates and screws in my damaged extremities were still where they belonged. "So, doc what are the damages", I muttered, he looked down at me and in his usual no nonsense manner said, "Bob you are one lucky young man, I only have to replace the leg cast which you crushed from the ankle on down". Looking up into the bright examination light, I softly said, "thank you God for watching over me and don't be too hard on my guardian angel, you know how rough he has it".

As the sound of the cast saw permeated the hospital room, I closed my eyes and fell fast asleep.

● ●● ● ● ●● ●●● ● ●●● ●● ● ● ● ●

There were moments in my life, that when the flurry of a day's activities had finally died down, a calming quiet would suddenly fill my inner soul. At times, I felt blessed to be able to feel Gods peace, it was in those moments of time that the spectacular nature of my creator's design would fill me with awe and wonder. One of those moments happened years ago, we were doing desert training at White Sands New Mexico, the arduous training began at O dark 30. As the sound of reverie floated through the air, young men quickly donned their camouflage BDU's, strapped on heavy rucksacks and grabbed their M16 rifles as they scrambled to get into formation. A quick breakfast at the white elephant and then a five-mile run to the range. The day's activities included small arms live fire practice, a two-man assault on a fortified position, a stint at the law rocket practice range, claymore mines, hand grenades and ending with a night time live fire event, which resulted in some impressive brush fires that required our immediate attention and our entrenching tools to squelch.

We then formed up into columns and began a long night's march through the sands of the desert. After walking into the wee hours of the next day, we finally halted and spread our sleeping bags out onto the sand covered ground and prepared our tired bodies for a much-needed rest. As I lay under that desert sky with no city lights to dim the heavens, I was suddenly amazed at all of the twinkling stars that filled the great dark expanse of space. How utterly beautiful was my heavenly view and yet how small and feeble it suddenly made me feel.

But yet in that moment, I also felt a warm and inviting closeness to God and that somewhere in that infinite blackness of space, a being of tremendous power loved this pitiful creature called me and as the dry desert winds began to pick up, those tiny particles of sand began to swirl and then began to sting my exposed flesh as if I had stepped on a hornet's nest. To end the painful assault, I zipped up my mummy sleeping bag so that only a small portal remained open, enough to keep most of the sand out and open enough to allow fresh air in. Within seconds, as the howls of coyotes pierced the chilled night, I fell soundly asleep.

The tubes inside the television began to glow with a yellowish hue, the speakers hissed and popped while a slight smell of ozone filled the air. Sitting crossed legged on the woolen carpet, I was clutching my imitation chromed pearl handled Mattel six shooters while also decked out in my Roy Rodgers pajamas, my black felt cowboy hat, and my white trimmed cowboy boots.

While sitting crossed legged, I waited with eager anticipation for the arrival of those black and white images which portrayed one my favorite cartoon characters. Waiting impatiently, the stern voice of my mother shattered my focused attention, "Bob don't sit so close to the tv set, you'll ruin your eye sight", "Okay mom", I answered back. After skootching back a mere few inches, I resumed by robotic gaze upon that flickering phosphorus screen.

The images, dim at first, suddenly popped up clear upon the magic tube, there was Wiley E Coyote opening a large box from the famous Acme Company, which, no doubt, contained the components of a, "damn, another commercial" I muttered. Just then my sister Gail entered the living room clutching her Barbie doll dressed in an evening gown. Without consultation, she walked confidently to the tuner, stuck her stinking butt in my face and to my chagrin, changed the channel.

In a child's world, that was akin to the medieval tradition of slapping someone's face with your glove announcing your intentions for a duel. "Mom Gail changed the channel", I screamed, "No I didn't", she responded back grinning, "Mom I was here first", I shouted back. "All right you two that's enough, Bob you need to get up and get dressed", Mom exclaimed. "God da__", hesitation, darnit", I retorted. Turning to face the object of my anger, I presented her with the I'm going to get you one of these day's facial expressions, her response, a shit eating grin followed up with sticking her tongue out. Uuuug, Sisters what good are they I thought as I headed for my room.

Now my dresser drawers were not the picture book examples of organization, as a matter of fact, it could take me two days just to find a matching pair of socks. It wasn't because my mother just threw my clothes into those wooden drawers wiley niley, she would place them into their proper places all neatly folded and then I would come along, and like a loosed pig rooting through the family garden, I would tear through those drawers as I searched for the days fashion.

[148]

Just as I had discovered a clean pair of underwear, in my sock drawer, an insistent knocking captured my attention. Looking out of the white laced curtains of the kitchen window, I saw my friend Louie standing on the side porch and searching for me through the doors window. "Mom, I'll get it", I shouted as I ran from my bedroom.

Opening the door, Louie looked me square in the eyes, grinned and said, "Mrs. Zierler can Bob come out and play", "Louie are you looking for a knuckle sandwich", I replied while giving him my best evil eye look. A momentary pause for effect and then we both burst into a round of laughter. "I was thinking" Louie said, "see right there, that's your problem, thinking", I retorted back, "I think it would be a good day to go to the park", he replied. "Mom is it alright if I go to the park with Louie", I screamed, "What" was her response over the sound of the vacuum cleaner, "can I go to the park with Louie", I shouted even louder. "Okay have fun, be safe and make sure you look both ways before you cross the street" she shouted back. "I'll be at your house in five minutes Louie, okay", I replied with a grin. "Sure, I'll be waiting" he replied as he leapt off our well-worn, paint peeling side porch.

As I recall, I didn't have my glossy black, twenty-six-inch Huffy bicycle yet so Louie and I hoofed it down Kenneth Avenue to La Follette Park.

As we approached the corner of Park Street and Kenneth Avenue, we saw the plethora of young heads bobbing up and down in the small rectangular pool looking like a pick a duck attraction at the annual Carnival.

As soon as the car turned the corner and passed our location, we broke into a run and without missing a step, dropped our towels at a close convenient location and then finding a small gap between the bobbing heads, we plunged in. The water, clear and powerfully chlorinated, felt warm but yet refreshing. The pool, I believe was only three or four feet deep at the deepest end of the pool, your chances of an actual drowning was extremely low, your chances of injury due to trampling was a touch higher. The first ten minutes or so was spent greeting familiar faces. With hair wet and faces dripping, it was our 1960's form of Facebook.

It was at this pool that I learned my first swimming stroke, the tried and true doggy paddle, previous to that skill, my swimming method consisted of diving into a body of water, didn't matter the depth, swimming underwater tadpole style, and coming up for an occasion breath of air, which always sent my grandmother or my mother into a complete state of hysterics which, of course, usually resulted in my receiving a red and sore bum.

The cacophony of laughter of those children's voices enjoying their play filled the park as we swam and chased each other gleefully around the pool's parameter.

Tired but happy, we would slowly walk back home allowing the heat of the summer sun to dry our wet hair and skin while the sound of barking squirrels marked our passage. Reaching home, Louie and I parted ways, "See yak after lunch Bob", he said, "I'll be waiting for you", I replied. The screech of the screen door announced my arrival and as Mom turned to face me, she said, "peanut butter and jelly for lunch?", "absolutely and heavy on the peanut butter please", I would playfully respond. The summer morning couldn't have been any better.

The warm tears rolled down my face as Gail requested to Mom that I had to attend yet another one of her tea parties, "but Mom tea parties are for girls", I sadly exclaimed. "Now Bob, Gail needs a guest for her party and seeing your younger sister isn't quite old enough yet, it'll have to be you", she responded. Without a word, tears rolling and nose sniffling, I walked over to her neatly prepared tea party table. As soon as I sat down, she began her tea party role playing, chatting excitedly about the current social events, while pouring her pretend tea into my red plastic cup. To this day, I still can't recall any of that conversation, to me it all sounded like, blah, blah, was, waaa, waaa. I do recall thinking that being tormented as a prisoner of war would be less uncomfortable than this, keep moving, hands on head, no talky, no talky.

The sound of red ball jet tennis shoes running up the steps of our front porch luckily signaled my much-needed liberation, "Mom Louie's here, we want to go back to the park", I hollered through the open living room window, "Okay, just be back before supper", she responded. Flipping off the napkin I had been required to wear, I jumped up and leapt over the railing of the porch, I was intensely feeling the joy of my new found freedom.

Louie and I ran a few blocks down Kenneth Avenue before we finally, huffing and puffing, slowed down. A few more blocks and the park suddenly loomed large before us and without hesitation, we headed for our first attraction, the dangerous, child spewing, merry go round.

We waited impatiently until the previous riders were finished and then we crawled up upon the multi colored circular structure perched upon a single post. When the riders had found their positions, one or two designated kids would begin pushing, turning the merry go round faster and faster. The surrounding landscape would begin to blur as it moved across our retinas in ever increasing speed. I loved that feeling. We hung on tighter and tighter as centrifugal force attempted to throw us off, crashing unto the grassy surface.

Our next adventure was on the two-kid merry go round, it had a small platform and a thick post that had two elongated handles welded to it. Either one or two kids would stand upon the platform and after a push to get it going, you could use your body weight to move it faster and faster. To this day, I know of no child that could withstand the amount of centrifugal force that ride provided. As it spun, the landscape would begin to rapidly blur and then your hands would begin to lose its grip and before you knew it, you were thrown clear of the ride, impacting the ground with an audible thud, unable to regain your feet until the vertigo in your head finally subsided. In today's world, that ride would be banned and labeled as cruel and unusual punishment, in our day it was a fun filled rite of passage.

The last event of the day were the swings. They consisted of thick leather seats that were suspended by heavy duty chain links. This wasn't your run of the mill backyard swing set, because as soon as you gained any altitude with the backyard variety, the legs would pull out of the ground thereby limiting your swing arc. On these park swings you could fly as high as you dared, the only limit to doing a full three-hundred-and-sixty-degree turn was the chain itself.

Sitting upon the leather seat, you would position your hands at the correct height and then with a slight push of your feet, the fun would begin. Pumping your arms and feet in an aggressive rhythmic fashion would propel you higher and higher, until you would reach that perfect point in your swing arc, where the chains would slacken and just at that right moment, before gravity would pull you back down, you would have that awesome feeling of weightlessness, that tickle feeling as your internal organs seemed to float up and then back down again, that feeling was pure joy.

Before we left for the day, we engaged in our swing set competition. We would take turns, swinging as high as we could and then launching yourself out of the swing at just the right forward height to achieve maximum distance. If you left to early, not enough distance, if you left to late, the butt numbing landing. Other kids would mark your landing spot and the child that had flew the farthest, was declared the day's winner.

We were sitting on the merry go round and talking just prior to going home. The sun was sitting low on the horizon, when an older man suddenly appeared in the front of us, wearing a long trench coat and without a word, he abruptly opened that long trench coat and in the wink of an eye, we were staring at the naked form of a middle-aged man. Staring back, he threw back his head and laughed, haa, haa, haa, haa. He then closed his trench coat and disappeared into the sunset. We named him the ha ha man, and it wasn't long until he was arrested for his exposure.

Walking back home as the sun drenched the horizon in its beautiful reds and oranges, it seemed to be the perfect ending for a perfect day at La Follette Park.

• • •• •• • • • • • •

I decided to write a few short stories of my life as a child to provide my future grandchildren and great grandchildren the opportunity to grasp a glimpse of who grandpa or great grandpa was, what it was like to grow up in my generation and the values that made me uniquely a child of God and a son of Bernard and Janet Zierler. I was a child filled with energy, curiosity and the inability to look before I leapt. This last trait resulted in a more the normal amount of physical pain and bloodletting, while generating moments of great anxiety and concern for my parents. I had often wondered during those growing and maturing years from childhood to adulthood how many extra guardian angels God had to provide just to see me through it.

My great passions in life are hunting, fishing, sports, friends and family. From the time I could remember, I was dragging Dad's guns through the house, he would always take out the bolts so there was no danger of an ugly and messy firearms accident and he would take the time to teach me the moral and physical responsibilities of handling firearms. I started learning the skills of archery at the age of six and became quite proficient at the ancient sport. The squirrels and chipmunks at my grandparent's cottage would scatter into hiding whenever they saw me and my trusty Bear recurve bow enter their realm. I bagged my first deer with the bow at the age of twelve and it provided me an activity that kept me out of trouble that other boys my age would become entangled in. And the wonderful hours spent with my grandfather, Richard Timmers, in his boat, lazily drifting across the diamond sparkled lakes of Wisconsin catching walleyes, perch, bass and northern pike, was a blessing bestowed by the Almighty and the patient tutelage of that kind and gentle grandfather.

These activities would have a strong and profound effect upon me tempering my views and values concerning the great outdoors, along with building such sweet and enjoyable memories with my male role models, my father and grandfather. They have crossed the river Jordan and have joined their family and friends in those gold mansions in the sky, many years ago already; but I can easily sit back and conjure up those special memories as though they had just happened yesterday.

I also had a great propensity and relish for sports such as, football, basketball, wrestling, baseball and boxing. I played these sporting activities with a lot of passion and energy. It taught me great values such

[153]

as, teamwork, discipline, concentration and good sportsmanship. Some of those values have been a marvelous benefit in my adult endeavors. You win some, you lose some, but you never stop learning and you never stop trying. That hard work and consistent effort, eventually produces your expected and desired results. That when you get the hell knocked out of you and you end up lying on your back, you pick yourself up by the bootstraps and get back into the game.

That an attitude of poor, poor pitiful me gets you nowhere nor anything substantial. That every day you wake up is a fresh beginning and the enjoyment you squeeze of every day is the result of one thing, your attitude. Your perspective can be either to look for the good and the joy that surrounds you or you can search for the negative and the ugly that also surrounds you. You choose to be positive or negative in your attitude towards others, events or life in general, it is not brought on by anyone else but you. Good and bad things happen to everyone, how you respond and how deeply you are affected, is the direct result of your attitude towards those events. I chose early in my life to wake up every morning thanking the Almighty above for yet another day, another opportunity to enjoy a beautiful day, whether the sun be a shining or heavy raindrop are falling from the sky.

The most important possessions you have are your values, standards, morality and a deep faith in your Creator. The world's values, standards and moralities are like a hurricane, prior to landfall, it is mesmerizing, intense and full of energy, but after it contacts mother earth, it leaves behind an immense path of death and destruction. The best and most peaceful days of my life, was when I accepted Christ into my heart, got on my knees and begged God for the forgiveness of my sins, which were plentiful and then began the intense search for God through the reading of his word, the bread of life, the bible. I found that by throwing away all of my previous biases from my religious upbringing and by reading the bible from front to back, book by book, chapter by chapter, verse by verse, keeping myself rooted in the subject and object of the verse, coupled with a good concordance that could bring the translation back to the Hebrew, Aramaic and Greek, I found more wisdom, joy, understanding and peace than at any other time in my life.

I have four segments of my life that I am the proudest of, they are my wife, my kids, my military service and my friends.

They have provided me with the most satisfaction and enjoyment than any other of my life's endeavors. I met my wife, your grandmother or great grandmother in a usual manner, especially in Wisconsin, where taverns far outnumber schools and churches. At that time of year, when the frigid winds of a Wisconsin winter begin to blow and the surrounding countryside is chilled to the consistency of ice. The most common activity is spending your nights at the local pubs, playing pool, darts or cards while dumping sparkling, piles of quarters into the glistening, chrome trimmed juke boxes. I was bartending for my mother, whom had just leased a second tavern in my home town, when a friend of mine, whom I had known for a few years, walked into the bar with the most beautiful girl I had seen in quite a while. As he walked down to his favorite corner of the bar, I began pouring his favorite beer, a glass of Miller Lite. As soon as he had sidled up to the bar, I placed the coaster on the bar and set upon it, his glass of foaming brew. I gazed at the pretty and well-shaped women standing next to him and without turning away my gaze, I asked him what his date wanted to drink, and his response was, emphatically, that's not my date, that's my sister. Yes, dear ones, upon hearing that response, I was as giddy as a young boy looking forward towards his first real kiss or that first slow dance with the cute freckled face, blue eyed beauty that sat ahead of me in grade school. It did not take me long to completely ignore Mike and concentrate my charms on his gorgeous sister. We fell into a rather comfortable and casual conversation;

I had noticed that she had driven to the tavern in a nice sports car, an Opel GT. And I asked her if the car was hers, she said no, but a friend of hers had let her use it for the night. After my shift was over, we walked up to another bar and sat at a table, in chairs directly across from each other and became deeply engulfed in getting to know each other better from that moment on, unknown to each of us, we would be spending the rest of our lives together, sharing the joys and the trauma's that life would throw our way. After enduring the trials and tribulations that every marriage goes through, we grew and nurtured a deep and lasting love, and a healthy respect for each other. She became my best friend, I shared everything with her, my dreams, my fears, my failures, my successes and hers with me, I believe with every fiber in my body, that our relationship was ordained by God himself. She is the mother of my three sons and is truly, a great blessing.

I grew up in an extended family that had served their country with pride and vigor. My dad served in the U.S Navy during World War II and spent four years chasing and fighting the Japanese throughout the pacific. He served aboard a diesel submarine and was responsible for keeping the engines aboard that vessel in good condition. I remember the stories he told me of the silent terror they experienced when a Japanese surface vessel was trying to end their patriotic duty with a barrage of depth charges. The submarine, at times, would settle on the bottom of the ocean and turn off the engines. This tactic would remove them from the enemy's radar screen. Dad said everyone on board the submarine would have to remain dead silent, any noise could be registered on the Japanese radar, pinpointing their position and enabling the enemy to destroy them quickly. He recalled that you could hear the timer ticking inside the depth charge and then a brief moment of silence when the timer ended, and then an explosion followed by a shock wave that violently rocked the submarine. He also described the beauty and wonder of the many pacific islands he had the opportunity to explore. In the last year of the war, dad was stationed in Perth Australia, awaiting the final invasion of the island of Japan. He absolutely loved Australia and eventually he fell in love with a local Australian woman.

On a clear, dark, but starry night, dad had taken his new found love to an outdoor amphitheater where they sat in bleachers and watched a Hollywood movie of the times. Upon walking back to the car, after the end of the movie, his wife to be was struck by a taxi driver and was killed. I cannot phantom the emotional trauma my dad endured after this horrible event. When he did talk of the accident years later, his eyes would well up with tears and his facial features would display a far-off appearance as if he was once again reliving that tragic event. His claim to combat fame occurred during a search and destroy mission. The submarine had surfaced during daylight hours to release the buildup of CO2 and replenish their oxygen supply. A Japanese Zero spotted the submarine and began to strafe the deck with its machine guns. Dad and a fellow sailor ran to the deck gun and began firing at the small Japanese fighter. After firing a few rounds at the highly maneuverable plane, they got lucky and actually hit the aircraft. They fished the Japanese pilot from the warm, shark infested, waters of the south pacific and placed him under guard inside the submarine. Dad said at first, the enemy pilot was terrified that the American sailors would brutally torture him and then in cannibal fashion, eat him. That was what the Japanese military was telling their military personnel, that the Americans were a brutal and cannibalistic lot. My dad and other sailors took turns guarding the pilot until they could finish the mission and turn him over the military police once they had returned to their submarine berth in Perth. Dad said they had treated the prisoner with compassion and kindness and after a while the Japanese pilot began to play cards with the sailors and perform duties such as washing dishes and doing laundry. By the time dad's submarine had anchored back in Perth, the Japanese pilot wanted to stay aboard with his new found friends and expressed a desire to be allowed to live in America and to not be returned to his homeland of Japan.

My dad's other brothers also served during World War II. His older brother and his younger brothers, except Louie who was too young at the time, served in the Army and the Army Air Corp in the European theatre. Louie Zierler, the baby of the family, served during the Korean conflict and was part of a mortar crew during the invasion of the Chinese across the Yangtze River which greatly escalated the duration and the human cost of the war.

I grew up listening to all the war stories supplied by my uncles and cousins. My grandmother's brother, Uncle Richard Baker, served in Patton's tank command and was one of the first tanks to cross the Rhine River during the battle of the Bulge. We used to watch a documentary that actually showed my uncles tank, engaging the German's guarding the bridge. His tank battled with machine gun nests and mortar rounds during the crossing and the capture of that key bridge, which the American Army would use to pour troops into Germany and ensure the final victory over Hitler's Nazi party and the German military forces.

I served in the U.S. Army for about eight years. I was a combat medic during my early service years and then took the Nuclear Medicine program taught by the U.S. Navy. I was proud of the medical service we provided those wounded soldiers who gave such a great sacrifice during the Gulf War. My unclaimed military opportunity came just before the end of my basic training. Out my company, ten of the best recruits, whom were recommended by the drill sergeants, were given the chance to join the fledging new unit called Delta Force. I was among that group of soldiers, I can still remember being marched to a facility that contained a conference room. Shortly after our arrival, a colonel entered the room and explained the mission of the newly formed Delta Force and we were given the general duties of that organization. It was to be a counter terrorism unit. We would be trained for a multitude of task, such as intelligence gathering, extractions, search and destroy and to be able to blend into hostile environments to be able to gather valuable ground intelligence. We would be allowed to grow our hair and beards and we would have to learn languages, weapons, explosives, and interrogation techniques. It was clearly spoken that it would be dangerous duty. I turned down that opportunity because Chris was expecting our first child and after wrestling with the glory of being a member of Delta Force or being available long term for my new family, I chose my family responsibility over the alluring patriotic call of joining an elite special forces unit. I do ponder at times if I had made the right decision and if I had decided differently, would I have had the opportunity to participate in critical missions that most service man only dream of. But then I look back in time and smile, knowing I would have missed huge chunks of time with my wife and with my three wonderful sons and then I know that I had made the right choice. And that right decision would lead me into my greatest adventure of all time, fatherhood.

I knew from an early age that I wanted to have children, lots of children. Whenever an infant came into view, I leapt at the opportunity to hold that infant and engage in making strange faces and cooing sounds to invoke from that infant a faint smile or an infectious baby laugh. I was always amazed at how a newly born baby who was completely incapable of existing on its own and would grow up, by stages, into a complex and independent adult. And when I met Chris, who had the same aspirations, the scene was set, we definitely were going to have kids but how many children was the only unanswered question. That answer came after we had Creg, our third son. I was still eager to continue mass producing the Zierler/Kamke prototypes, but Chris, being the financial officer of the family, rapidly came to the conclusion that we really could not afford any more children, especially on the salary of a Sergeant in the Unites States Army.

This brings me to a humiliating and a cowardly event in my life. After my wife had decided not to bear anymore rug rats, curtain climbers or ankle biters, she asked if I would get a vasectomy. That one phrase brought out a side of me that I did not know existed at the time. It invoked a feeling of fear that I believe only fire fighters trapped inside a burning high-rise experience. Now, I have had done lots of male macho military training and exercises up to this point, even the thought of getting shot, losing a limb or being shredded by shrapnel did not invoke the same sense of dread. The mere cranial image of a doctor's somewhat shaky hand, poised, ready to start carving on the twin's was unbearable. I even, went to visit a friend of mine who just had a vasectomy done by one of the base doctors. I knocked on the door and was greeted by a feeble and pain edged voice saying, 'come on in'. I walked into the living room and there on the couch was my friend sitting, in a T-shirt and a pair of socks. Yes, you heard me right, just a T-shirt and a pair of socks, holding the biggest bag of frozen peas upon his obscured scrotum. I faintly remember asking him how he was doing, what I truly and vividly remember, was the groan followed by him uncovering his scrotum and seeing the most swollen, black and blue set of twins I had ever in my life, and believe me I had friends kicked in the crotch so hard they had passed out from the blow, been witness too. It was at that point that the yellow streak began to rapidly course up the length of my spine and I could not bring myself to have the vasectomy that my wife was pleading with me to have. She opted instead, to have her tubes tied, which I did discover through some lengthy research, was not as painful as a vasectomy. But none the less, whenever I would start bragging about my sports past or my military past with too much bravado and testosterone, my wife would always bring up this delicate and humiliating event of my life, which would always settle me down into a humbler posture.

I was blessed with four children, my first wife and I had a daughter, her name is Andria, she is married and now has the last name of Bena. She graduated from college with a degree in Psychology, and what a useful career, especially, in dealing with me. I have always loved her very much, but at the same time, I have carried the guilt of not always being there for her when she was growing up. He mother and I divorced when I she was five. And when I entered the service, the economy was down and jobs in the fox valley were hard to find. The service allowed me the opportunity to provide for her and my new family. But despite that setback, she became lovely, loving and intelligent young women, with a strong sense of family and values. With my second wife, Chris, we had three sons with the names of David, Justin and Creg. I was allowed to name the first-born son, so I picked the name David, as a child, I was always enamored by the bible story of David and Goliath. How David, a shepherd, almost still a boy, slew the giant with one well-placed stone from his sling shot. The other two sons were named by my wife, Chris. Why I mentioned that, I really do not know, maybe that was the start of the power struggle that always occurs in marriages. Who handles the money, who makes the decisions, who controls the bedroom, hint, hint, and who consistently sleeps on the couch after an argument. But being a father and the experiences of becoming a father was everything I had ever imagined it to be.

When they were infants, I would participate in the daily activities of rearing children, changing diapers, warming bottles, pacing to and fro or rocking them for hours in the middle of the night or rushing them to the doctor's office or the emergency room when they were sick or in pain. I used to love taking knaps with them on the weekends, I would, at times, just lay with them and stare at their tiny facial features and fingers. And

[159]

be consumed with the awe and the miracle of it all. When they became toddlers, I would love to get down on the floor and play with them or chase them around the house, listening to the delightful sound of their giggles and squeals. I would, almost every night when I was home, get them all snuggled into one bed and then I would let them choose a children's book for me to read. Chris and I had a discussion and had decided that the ability to read and comprehend was one of the most important aspects of education. And we were going to immerse them in the world of words and imagination. I had a habit of changing the story line, usually telling the story in a more humorous manner. This was done to illicit laughter from my children, God how I loved to hear their sound of their laughter. But, at times, it would begin to backfire on me.

On those nights, after a long, long, work day, I would want to just read the book and then put myself to bed. After a few pages, my kids would all begin to interject, pleading for me to think up a new and funny story line, it was difficult, but the end result was always worth the effort. It is a miracle to watch your children grow from an infant, who is completely dependent upon you for their very survival, to an intelligent, honest, hard working, moral and independent adult. I cannot express how much I love my children and how proud I am of all of them. They have been my greatest achievement and have provided more joy than any other accomplishment in my life, except for my relationship with their mother, my wife, my best friend.

My work history is a patch work of blue collar, military and corporate careers. My first paying job was working on one of the numerous dairy farms that dotted the landscape outside of my home town. I was twelve years old and I was baling hay. I made two cents a bale, now that may not sound like a lot of money, but at that time, you could buy candy for a penny apiece. I also got my first lesson in driving a farm tractor, which I did with great relish and great peril to anyone standing nearby. I remember that the clutch spring was so strong that I had to stand up and place all of my weight on the clutch pedal to depress it sufficiently enough to shift the tractor into a different gear. My next gig was working at the local Piggly Wiggly grocery store. I would bag groceries and stock shelves.

It taught me a working trait that has been a benefit to me and to every job I have worked at since, that trait was great customer service. Bill Verhagen, who was running the store, was extremely adamant at developing that trait in every employee. Even when the old hag was whining and screaming at you because you were using bags instead of boxes or was not bagging her groceries in her own confusing standard, we had to reply with a smile and a yes ma-am or a yes sir and proceed to satisfy their every crazy whim. "The customer is always right", he would say after a particular difficult bagging event and it's the customer who is really paying your check. I have used that philosophy whether working on the assembly lines of manufacturers or conducting interviews of corporate employees for important business analysis that would be used in my computer programming. I started, after high school, to work for the same company my father, grandfather, uncles and friends worked for, which was Thilmanys Paper. I only lasted about a year, the rotating shift work, the long sixteen-hour days, when your partner failed to show up for work, and working on the weekends, gradually wore me down. I quit Thilmanys and started work at Giddings and Lewis, a company that manufactured machine shop equipment. From grinders, to drill presses, to lathes, and other commercial grade machine shop equipment. I really liked working there, you were assigned a constant shift, either days, which was from 6:00 am to 3:00 pm or nights, which was from 3:00 pm to 11:00 pm and no weekends. It fit right in with my active social schedule, like drinking beer on Friday night, Saturday night and Sunday afternoon.

With the occasional weekend excursion to the beach or to grandpa's cottage on Crooked Lake thrown in. I hate to admit or even think about the amount of money I spent either drinking or chasing skirts, but I am sure it would have funded any retirement account quite nicely. That job lasted three years until the economy slowed down and a rather large group of us were eventually laid off. My next career choice was construction. I started working as a mason tender for a company called Miller Masonry. It was great, especially for a young man, the hard physical labored kept me in great shape and the ability to work outside was also great for my skin, especially in its ability to produce large amounts of melanin, which resulted in a fantastic tan. For the next five years I did all kinds of construction work, from pouring foundations, basement walls, sidewalks and driveways; to working with contractors building custom homes for clients, where I learned the skill of carpentry. The only downside to construction work in Wisconsin, if you consider it a downside, was we got laid off every winter, kind of hard to dig a basement when the ground is frozen solid. The weekly routine during the layoff was to pick up our unemployment check and spend the rest of the week ice fishing in the mornings and hitting the bars at night, this I did when I was single.

But the wheels of restlessness were beginning to grow, I loved the construction work, but I also noticed that the older guys who were still in construction suffered from a variety of job-related medical problems. Which were bad backs, bad knees, arthritic fingers and a host of other maladies that seemed to plaque these men. It was then that I started to think that construction work was not the proper long term career choice for me. Shortly after, I matriculated at the University of Wisconsin and studied pre-med. My plan was to become a Chiropractor. I had been seeing Dr. Bill Haanen, a great chiropractor, during my football years at the high school. We struck up a pretty good friendship and after a construction accident which damaged my back, he convinced to me to go to school for chiropractic and after graduation, he would allow me to partner with him in his flourishing practice. I had completed the two years of pre-med that was a prerequisite for chiropractic school, and had been accepted at Logan School of Chiropractic.

I was married to my first wife then, Paula Zettel, it was at this moment in my life when she decided that our marriage was over and sued for a divorce. Andria was only about three or four years old at that time. I had to turn down my acceptance at Logan Chiropractic School and return back to work so I could fulfill my child support obligations. For a period of time after the divorce, I worked mostly has a bartender for my mother who was leasing two taverns in my home town of Kaukauna WI. It was there that I met Chris Kamke, my future wife and best friend. We ended up leasing a bar of our own in a small rural town in Wisconsin called Chilton. I must have been drunk when I agreed to the lease contract because when I sobered up and was standing outside the bar looking at it, I noticed that the whole building had a substantial lean to the right. We named the beer pouring establishment, Bob's Log Cabin, it really did have log siding on the exterior of the structure and opened it for business. Being strangers in a small rural town definitely has it business challenges. There was another drinking establish just around the corner from our place, and it was run by a popular local high school graduate. Trying to pull customers from that business was akin to a dentist trying to extract the molars from a wolverine, without any anesthesia. Within a year, we were starting to have problems paying the bills and it was then, on a fine autumn morning, that I walked across the street to the Chilton recruiting office and joined the Army. Besides marrying Chris, joining the service was another smart choice. It provided three squares, that's meals to you civilians, training and college benefits. The Army paid off my first two years of student loans and provided the funding for my

System Analyst/Computer Programmer career, which I obtained after I had left the military service.

I hope these few stories that I have shared with you, gives you a glimpse of what grandpa or great grandpa, etc., Robert Zierler was like. It is a shame that after a few generations, we lose who our ancestors were, their names, and their lives. If you close your eyes and imagine really hard, you are alive because your ancestors were successful at bearing and rearing children for thousands of years. So many have come before us and so many will pass afterwards but that is the circle of life. It has been my pleasure to provide you with the means to obtain life, and remember it's not the number of years we have, but how we live the years we have been given. Enjoy your life, rise to the challenges that life will bring your way, never give up hope.

Arise each day with the knowledge that you have the chance and the choice to begin anew, to be happy, to help a neighbor or a friend, to enjoy the sound and sights of nature, to give your spouse or your children a hug, a kiss and a smile. To know that true happiness is found within us, not outside of us. When we come to terms with our self, to learn to like ourselves, to be comfortable with who we are, to establish our own identities by the morals and values that are important to you, not what the group, the cliché or your peers what you to have and to own. That God created you a unique individual, with your own fingerprints, your own DNA, your own personality. And he gave you gifts that are best suited for you, that will bring you enjoyment and contentment that nobody else can provide for you.

When you finally arrive at that place, the joy of life will radiate out of you like light from the sun. People will automatically be attracted to you; your positive attitude and your friendly optimism will draw others like a moth to a lamp. And remember this, it is not a sin to be poor, but it is a sin to stay poor. Unless, you are truly handicapped, God expects to you to utilize and to nurture the talents he has blessed you with. To work for your bread, God promises to bless your work as long as your work is legitimate and honestly obtained. God does not say he will bless you while you are sitting on your ass and whining and complaining. So, get up and research a career path that will provide adequately for you and your family. Now that is going to take, sacrifice, dedication and some sweat, but the end result will be a skill that companies or people are ready and willing to pay for. And that does not always mean college, a good trade such as, heating and cooling, plumbing or electrical plus a host of other trade skills will also provide you with a valuable skill set.

[163]

Learn to balance your life between work, family and friends and yes, it is alright to spend a little time with yourself doing what you enjoy. I loved to hunt and fish, I relished the challenge of the pursuit, but I also loved those times when the sun was just coming up and I could witness the woods or lake come to life. The nocturnal animals were saying their goodnights and the daytime animals were beginning to stir. It was at those times that I would feel a special bond with God's creation and a closeness with God himself.

Remember, the past helps defines our present and anchors us into the journey of the unknowing future. Like history, it is ever changing and shaping our destiny. I have been blessed with a wonderful wife, kids and grandchildren.

To my grandchildren, whom I dearly love

Learn from your failures, for they are just a few lessons away from your successes. You will have profound moments of happiness mingled with some trials and tribulations, remember those trials and tribulations are what build your character and they help to hone your values. Honor, love and respect your parents, why, because they gave you your physical existence. Also, honor, love and respect God, because he gave you your soul, that is what makes you unique, learn to guard it and protect it, it is up to you to maintain its everlasting status. How? By searching for God through reading his word, the bible, that is how you learn to guard it and to protect it.

Goodbye
    and
I love you all.
Robert Alan Zierler

A SHORT FAMILY TREE

Roberts Tree
Richard Timmers   Dorothy Baker

                Janet Timmers

Frank Zierler   Frieda Schacher

                Bernard Zierler

Bernard Zierler   Janet Timmers

                Robert Zierler
                Gail Zierler
                Debbie Zierler
                Mary Zierler

Chris's Tree
Bernard Rolf   Ethel DeKuster
                Mardell Rolf

Frank Kamke   Cecilia Manlich

                Raymond Kamke

Raymond Kamke   Mardell Rolf
                Mike Kamke
                Mark Kamke
                Christine Kamke
                Jeff Kamke

Robert Zierler   Paula Zettel
                Andria Zierler

Robert Zierler   Chris Kamke
                David Zierler

Justin Zierler
Creg Zierler

Andria Zierler   Jim Bena
Kate Bena
Allison Bena

Creg Zierler   Amanda Bishop
Naomi Zierler
Aden Zierler
Julia Zierler

P.S.

As the sun sets and begins to shed its brilliant tentacles of oranges and reds, I lay resting on the hotel couch after a hard day's work. I am eight hundred miles from home and alone. The soft glow of the television and the sounds of an unfamiliar movie are my companions, my respite. In these moments, when encompassed by strangers and strange surroundings, is where memories are suddenly loosed to fly around the recesses of your mind as surely as a butterfly which has shed the confinement of its cocoon and is flying constantly and frantically around the emitting glow of a light. The memories that I cherish the most are those of my children, the beautiful sound of their laughter, the warm and comfortable naps taken together on a lazy weekend afternoon. Laying in bed with the three of them snuggled up against my sides, staring at me with eyes wide with the anticipation of the story I was about to tell. Watching them slowly grow from dependant loving children into mature and responsible adults. It is then that I am acutely aware of God's blessing and mercy. And the answer to a prayer I had uttered years ago during a very painful episode of my life. To say that I am a very lucky man is a grave misunderstanding. For truly, the real answer is that I have been a very blessed man and for that, eternally grateful.